T0146927

A NEW World IS Coming!

REVISED EDITION

ROBIN LOUISE

WESTBOW
PRESS®
A DIVISION OF THOMAS NELSON
& ZONDERVAN

WestBow Press books may be ordered through booksellers or by contacting:

WestBow Press
A Division of Thomas Nelson & Zondervan
1663 Liberty Drive
Bloomington, IN 47403
www.westbowpress.com
844-714-3454

ISBN: 979-8-3850-0873-5 (sc)
ISBN: 979-8-3850-0874-2 (hc)
ISBN: 979-8-3850-0875-9 (e)

Library of Congress Control Number: 2023918846

Print information available on the last page.

WestBow Press rev. date: 10/24/2023

This book is written for those people who believe in Jesus Christ as the Son of God, for those who want to believe that there is a God and aren't sure what to believe in, but most of all for the glory of our Lord and His kingdom.

Contents

Preface

People want to believe that there is something more than being asleep once you die. They have hope that maybe there is a heaven and they get to live there and not hell. Some people may not even believe there is a hell. The Bible tells of different levels of hell: outer darkness, bottomless pit, the abyss, and the lake of fire. If you are taking the time to read this book in hopes of finding answers to what life will be like after death or after the Battle of Armageddon, then you want to believe that there is life after death—and there is.

A new world is coming. A world that will be different from the way you see it now. It will be a better world and a much better place to live. This is because Jesus, the Son of God, will be Ruler and King here on earth. After the Battle of Armageddon when Satan is defeated by Christ, God's dwelling place, called the New Jerusalem, will come down from the clouds and settle here on earth. The New Jerusalem is the dwelling place of God and His people. Christ will rule from His Throne here on earth. There will be people who survive and live through God's wrath who will be ruled by Christ Himself. If you do not want to go through God's wrath or die and end up in a place of hell, then you need to know the signs of when the Lord is coming again. You need to be prepared for His coming, so you are taken out by the Lord before His wrath begins and ends with the Battle of Armageddon.

Remember what happened during Noah's time. People ignored and laughed at Noah when he was building the ark. The only ones who survived were Noah and his family because they believed, had faith in what God told them, and prepared. When the rains came, the people all wanted to get on board that ark. However, when the door of the ark was shut, no one could get in. The same will happen when Christ comes for His people. He will take them into His chambers and shut the door. No one who isn't taken at His Second Coming will get in.

I have written this book to share with you the information I have accumulated over the years from studying the Bible on my own and learning from others. I am not telling you these things to be what some may call a "doomsdayer." This is not my intention. My intentions are to save you from going through God's wrath and—worse—not making it to heaven. Those people who are not taken when our Lord comes for those who love Him, live trying to follow Him, and accepted Jesus as their Lord and Savior, will be left behind to encounter the most horrendous hardships and sufferings ever known to humankind. God's wrath will be poured out upon the earth after He takes His chosen ones out. People from all nations—Jews and Gentiles, including Protestants and Catholics, who include our family members, friends, and loved ones—will need hope, strong will, and encouragement to help them survive through the greatest tribulation that's ever been. I pray that by giving you some insight of the life you will have in the new world to come you will embrace faith, which will allow you to enter the kingdom of God. I want you to have a better life today, tomorrow, and in the hereafter. I pray that after you are done reading this book you will have some understanding of what is to come and how you can prepare for Christ's coming. Then if you still don't believe, as time goes on and these events come to pass, you will believe and know what you need to do.

The Holy Bible tells us that Jesus is going to come for His people at the end of this age and create a new heaven and a new earth. The Lord has given me an urgency to inform people of what there is to look forward to, providing they choose to live for righteousness and live for God. People go about life doing their own thing without having any regard for God's will, living for themselves, their own way, and not living for God. They don't know or understand God or know what He expects from them. They might believe in His existence, but they don't know Him. People just don't realize the consequences they will face in not making the choice to live for Him now before He comes to deliver His people from God's wrath upon the earth.

My strongest desire is to give you knowledge of what you will have if you are allowed to enter through the gates of heaven, what life will be like in paradise, and what it'll take to get there. God only asks for us to live for Him now. However, if you're left behind after He comes for the people who have been waiting and watching for His coming, you will then have to die for Him. You will have to suffer through God's wrath—the most severe hardship, disease, and catastrophic destruction that has ever taken place upon this earth. And worse, you might not enter through the gates of heaven in the new world. Only those who remain loyal to God and proclaim Jesus Christ as their Lord and Savior will enter heaven. However, God does not want anyone to perish; God wants you to have everlasting life with Him. God wants you to know that He has created the most glorious, unimaginable place for us to dwell in. Soon there will be a new heaven and a new earth. A new world is coming!

Introduction

Many people wonder and have doubts about the authenticity of the Word of God, the Holy Bible. They are not sure how much of the Bible is truly from God, or was it really God's thoughts written by man? Also, what Bible or religion is the true Word of God? After all, there are many different religions around the world that all profess their god and Bible is the one and only true way to heaven. However, there is only *one* true Living God: the God of Abraham, Jacob, and Isaac.

There are many scholars who have done extensive studies and written books on finding the answers to these questions. Out of all religions and various Bibles that have been written, it has been found that every one of them has flaws, except for the original scriptures that were commissioned by King James to be translated into English. Some Bibles have been revised from the King James Version for easier reading and understanding, such as the New International, Living Bible, and Revised Standard. But they are still the Word of God.

You might ask yourself, "How do these scholars know how to make this decision? How do they know what God, a Spirit that we cannot see or physically speak to, has spoken? And what scriptures were God inspired?" The answer is very simple. There are no flaws or errors in God's Word. God created the magnificent universe we live in with perfection. Therefore, His Word would also be written with perfection. Although the physical design of man was created with perfection, man himself is not perfect. Man makes choices due to what he has been taught and experienced. Man makes decisions and acts upon his knowledge or even theory of what he knows at that point in time. Sometimes it's good; sometimes it's not so good.

The Holy Bible was written by men who had no understanding or knowledge of the prophecies they were writing about. They did not understand what they were writing because most of it wasn't meant to be understood until a later time. The Bible is full of prophecies that have already come to pass and some that are yet to come. Some scriptures were explaining what had taken place, just as man has recorded history from the beginning. Most of all, the scriptures were telling us how we are to be living out our lives, how to treat one another, and how to be successful in our personal lives, but foremost, they tell us how to love and worship God.

These various ranks of men throughout the Holy Bible lived in distant places from each other, at various times in history, and had no means of communication with each other. From the time of Moses, who wrote the first scriptures, to the apostle John, who wrote the Book of Revelation 1,600 years later, the Bible was written in three different languages on three different continents. The scriptures were written by these men who lived in the desert, the wilderness, a palace, tropical paradise, on a barren island, and in a cave. These separate holy scriptures were written by two kings, two priests, a doctor, two fishermen, two shepherds, a pharisee, a politician, a tax collector, a soldier, a scribe, and a butler. Yet the Bible is a continuous message and account of the history of God's creation, from the inception of the human race all the way to our eternal presence around the throne of God. It is an indescribable event of what was, what is, and what is to come.

The men who wrote the scriptures wrote of things that they had no scientific knowledge of at that time. Bibles from religions that do not follow the original scriptures or translated scriptures from the King James Version were not written by men who were inspired by God. They contain errors and speculations, which are common to men and do not have the true knowledge or scientific facts that have been proven throughout time. For example, the Hindu scriptures said the moon was higher than the sun and that the moon shines by its own light, having luminous qualities. Ancient Hindu scriptures also stated that the world was flat and the whole mass rests on countless elephants. When the elephants shake, it produces earthquakes. The Hindus speculated, which is what we do when we don't understand. The Koran stated that the stars were lit torches in the heavens and people were baked clay. However, there are no speculations with the Holy Bible; it is God's Word.

Job stated that the moon had no luminous qualities of its own long before scientists declared it.

The book of Psalms says the sun is on its own course in the heavens and scientists laughed because they thought for years that the sun revolved around the earth. Just recently, scientists discovered the sun is on its own path circulating throughout the universe in a huge orbit pulling the entire solar system with it.

Jeremiah said the stars were innumerable, while man speculated throughout history there were only hundreds.

Moses insisted on following a regiment for antibacterial hygiene 3,500 years before scientists saw bacteria.

Jonah described underwater mountain ranges, while the world believed the ocean floor was a flat, sandy bowl.

Solomon talked about underwater springs feeding the ocean, when the world believed the oceans were only fed by rivers and rainwater.

Moses described the explosive birth of the universe thousands of years before Albert Einstein was born.

Genesis tells of the entire earth being flooded by water. Archaeologists have recently discovered whale fossils on Mount Ararat, the highest peak on earth, verifying that the earth was completely covered by ocean water at one time.

Evidence shows us that the Holy Bible *is* the true Word of God. The various books throughout the Old Testament and New Testament, covering a period of over 6,000 years, stated predictions that have come to pass and some that are yet to come. Man could learn so much about life and the world in which we live today and our eternal life and world that is to come, if we would only have faith in the one and only true Living God.

One
BE WATCHFUL

———— ∞∞∞ ————

For you to come to know God and understand what He expects from you, you need to know and understand His Word. Many people find that this is hard to do, seeing the Holy Bible is long and, in many aspects, difficult to understand. Yet the scriptures are very explicit and complete; some scriptures were not to be understood until God's specific timing. Well, the timing is now to understand what you need to know so you are not one of those left after Christ's Second Coming, known as the rapture. The rapture is referring to the event when we who are alive and remain will be caught up together with those who have died believing in Christ in the clouds to meet the Lord in the air (1 Thess. 4:17 NKJ).

The Lord has prompted me to present His Word to you with an easy reading style for better understanding and comprehension of God's message.

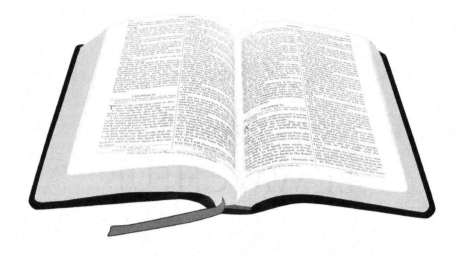

The Holy Bible is a gathering of several books that were written by different authors over several thousands of years. The Bible is separated into two sections: the Old Testament, which addresses the period from the creation of the heavens, the earth, and man to right before the birth of Christ, and the New Testament, which addresses the period from Christ's birth to the end of this world, the destruction of this earth, and the beginning of the new heaven and earth.

Although the Bible describes several events, tells stories of many different lives, and includes prophecies of what is to come, the basic theme of the Holy Bible is very simple and is constant: God created man in His image for man to be like Him, to have love, and to live in righteousness.

After God sent Adam and Eve, God's first creation of man, out of the Garden of Eden, God left our world in a state of sin, not living the way God wanted for thousands of years, waiting for humankind to choose between evil and good. When God sent Adam and Eve out of the Garden of Eden, He put angels (cherubim) with a flaming sword that flashed back and forth on the east side to keep them from the tree of life. At His appointed time, God will reclaim the earth, stars, and all the heavens and claim all as His forever and ever. Satan will no longer have dominion over the earth, as God will change the world back to the way He wanted it to be in the beginning, before Adam and Eve ate from the Tree of Knowledge.

God will destroy this earth and create a new earth. When God does create this new world for us, only those who have chosen to be His people will be allowed to enter His kingdom—those who chose to live by His Word. Jesus said that not everyone will enter the kingdom of heaven, but only those who do God's will.

At His first coming, Jesus Christ came as a man. God manifested in the flesh. He came to save humankind from sin because to die in sin is to die forever. The only way you can live forever is by removing sin through belief in Jesus. If you accept Jesus Christ as the Son of God who died for your sins, your sins will be forgiven through this gift of grace. Then you can enter the kingdom of God.

You cannot enter the kingdom of God in a state of sin. God doesn't want anyone to perish and be condemned to hell forever. He sent His Son, Jesus Christ, to save the world from their sins and have everlasting life in heaven. If you accept and believe in Christ as the begotten Son of God, your sins will be forgiven. Therefore, you will not die in sin and will live forever. God loves the world so much that He sent His only Son, Jesus, hoping that people would believe in Him and not perish and have eternal life.

Not all men rejoiced over Christ's first coming and the good news He brought with Him. Men rejected the only begotten Son of God and hung Him on a cross until He died. But they did not truly kill Jesus and the good news He brought. Jesus Christ, the Son of God, rose three days later. And the good news He brought remains and is offered to every man, woman, and child: believe in Him and you will have eternal life. After Jesus rose from the tomb, His resurrection, Christ gave the disciples His great commission to go and teach God's Word to everyone. Christ's great commission to people was for them to teach the world His Word, the good news, and how to be saved. The good news is that whoever believes in Him and is baptized will be saved and not condemned. Jesus said He will come for His elect, those people chosen because they believed in Him and want to have everlasting life with Him in heaven. Before He was crucified, Jesus said,

> Immediately after the tribulation of those days the sun will be darkened, and the moon will not give its light; the stars will fall from heaven, and the powers of the heavens will be shaken. Then the sign of the Son of man will appear in heaven, and then all the tribes of the earth will mourn, and they will see the Son of man

coming on the clouds of heaven with power
and great glory. And he will send out his angels
with a loud trumpet call, and they will gather
his elect from the four winds, from one end of
heaven to the other. (Matt. 24:29–31 NKJ)

Jesus Christ is coming for those who believe in Him as
the Son of God, those who are still alive and those who
have died. Those who die in Christ will arise from the
dead, just as Christ rose up after His death by crucifixion.
Then those chosen who are alive will rise up with them
and together meet the Lord in the air; this is known as the
rapture. Although we do not know the hour or the day our
Lord will come, we are not to be ignorant of His coming. We
are to be watchful and be children of light and not live in the
darkness of deception. The Lord tells us to be watchful for
His Second Coming. Immediately thereafter, the wrath of
God takes place on those left behind, ending with the Battle
of Armageddon.

People are not to be ignorant about those who have died
or even grieve like those living who have no hope. This is
because we know that Jesus died and rose up from the dead
and will bring all those who died believing in Christ with
Him. God's Word says that those who are alive at His Second
Coming, also known as the day of the Lord, will not be taken
until after the dead in Christ are taken up first. So when you
hear the trumpet call of God, look up to heaven because the
Lord Himself will be calling loudly as an archangel. Then

you will see the dead in Christ rise up to heaven. Afterward, all those who are still alive and believe in Christ will then be caught up in the clouds to meet with them and the Lord in the air. And forever we will be with the Lord.

God says that you should know the times and seasons. He will come when people say there is peace and safety, but then sudden destruction will come upon them just like a woman who is about to give birth. However, they will not escape. Jesus said you should not be surprised because you are sons of light and not of darkness.

There are many reasons needing to be watchful for the Lord's coming. You should be prepared and be teaching others how and why they need to be prepared. Do you not teach your children how to protect themselves from thieves, murderers, and rapists? Do you teach them not to do certain things that are not good for them? How to maintain a healthy lifestyle? In the same manner, you need to be teaching your loved ones and friends how to protect themselves from the evil one who leads us away from God.

In the last days, before Christ's Second Coming, Satan will work even harder at leading you astray. He tricks you into believing in him because he knows his time is short; the Lord will conquer him at the Battle of Armageddon. During the end of days, Satan will present himself as a man doing great things in order to get you to believe in him and not God. This great deceiver is called the Antichrist because he is against Christ. He will mimic the same actions as Christ, such as the following:

- He will perform strange demonstrations.
- He will do miracles.
- He will die and come back to life.
- He will want people to worship him.

Although people will be forced to worship the Antichrist, Jesus gives you the choice to worship God of your own free will. The Antichrist sets out to conquer and achieve world power and will deceive many—all those who did not know what to look for or expect.

> This man of sin will come as Satan's tool, full of satanic power, and will trick everyone with strange demonstrations, and will do great miracles. He will completely fool those who are on their way to hell because they have said "no" to the Truth; they have refused to believe it and love it, and let it save them, so God will allow them to believe lies with all their hearts, and all of them will be justly judged for believing falsehood, refusing the Truth, and enjoying their sins. (2 Thess. 2:9–12 LB)

We need to be watchful just as we are watchful with our daily lives. We lock our doors when we leave the house because we are concerned that thieves will come in and steal our personal treasures. Robberies happen when we least expect them. In the same way, we need to be prepared for the Lord's coming. For the Lord will come when we least expect Him.

Since you do not know the day our Lord is coming, you need to be watchful. If you knew at what time in the night a thief was coming to break into your house, you would be watching and not let anyone break into your home. Hence, you must also watch and be ready for the Son of man will come at an hour you least expect. If you are a faithful and wise servant of God who has been put over his household, you should be giving that household food at the proper time. God will bless that servant when He comes and finds him doing so. God will surely put that servant over all his possessions. However, if you are not a good servant and say that you do not know why your Lord is slow in coming, and you abuse your fellow servants and eat and drink with the drunkards, your Lord will come on a day and hour you do not expect. You will be punished and put with the hypocrites, where you will be weeping and gnashing your teeth with them (Matt. 24:42–51 RSV).

Ezekiel 33:1–6 explains that it is necessary to be watchful for others as well. You are responsible for telling others what you know about the Lord's Second Coming. If you tell others and they do not want to listen, then you tried and the burden of what is to come is not on you. They are rejecting the Truth. The Lord expects us to inform others of dangers and the struggles that are coming. The end-time tribulation, and especially the great tribulation, will be extremely difficult to live through. However, they will have a chance to protect themselves, prepare for what is to come, and survive through the difficulties that are to come. If that person does not want to know and ignores you and harm is inflicted upon him, his grievance is his own doing.

Even though no one knows the day or hour our Lord will return for His people, we are to be wise and watch for His coming or you will be left behind. Those people left behind will encounter God's wrath, the greatest hardship the world has ever known, the destruction of humankind, and this world.

God says no one knows the exact day or hour when the day of the Lord will come. But you will know the season. It will be just like in the days of Noah. Before the flood came, people were living their lives having parties, getting married, all the way until the flood came upon them and Noah entered the ark. People laughed and mocked at Noah and his family for preparing for this flood. They knew it was coming. It is believed that the ark took years to build, and it was 510 feet long, eighty-five feet wide, and fifty-one feet high. Plus they gathered tons of food for themselves and the animals. This is the same it will be at the Lord's Second Coming. You know the time is near; therefore, you need to keep watch and stay alert.

The most important reason for being watchful and prepared is so you will be ready when the Lord comes for His people and not left to endure God's wrath on humankind for not listening and wanting to be with Him. Christ is coming to get first those who are asleep and died believing in Him and then those who are alive who love Him and want to be with Him. Jesus is soon coming for His bride!

Two
THE WEDDING FEAST

The Lord refers to those who have been faithful and believed in Him as His bride. At His Second Coming, Christ will take His bride up to heaven at the *rapture* for the wedding feast. In order to understand the wedding feast and the parable of the ten bridesmaids in Matthew 25, you need to have understanding of the Jewish wedding custom.

The betrothal was binding and could only be undone by a divorce with proper grounds, such as the bride being found not to be a virgin. (See the story of Joseph and Mary in Matthew 25:1–13.) The young man prepared a *ketubah*, or marriage contract (covenant), which he presented to the intended bride and her father. Included in this was the "bride price," which was appropriate in that society to compensate the young woman's parents for the cost of raising her as well as being an expression of his love for her.

To see if the proposal was accepted, the young man would pour a cup of wine for his beloved and wait to see if she drank it. This cup represents a blood covenant. If she drank the cup, she would have accepted the proposal and they would be betrothed. The young man would then give gifts to his beloved and take his leave. The young woman would have to wait for him to return and collect her. Before leaving, the young man would announce, "I am going to prepare a place for you," and "I will return for you when it is ready." The usual practice was for the young man to return to his father's house and build a honeymoon room there. This is what is symbolized by the *chuppah* or canopy, which is characteristic of Jewish weddings. He was not allowed to skimp on the work and had to get his father's approval before he could consider it ready for his bride. If asked the date of his wedding, he would have to reply, "Only my father knows."

Meanwhile, the bride would be making herself ready so that she would be pure and beautiful for her bridegroom. During this time, she would wear a veil when she went out to show she was spoken for (she had been bought with a price).

When the wedding chamber was ready, the bridegroom

could collect his bride. He could do this at any time so the bride would make special arrangements. It was the custom for a bride to keep a lamp, her veil, and her other things beside her bed. Her bridesmaids were also waiting and had to have oil ready for their lamps.

When the groom and his friends got close to the bride's house, they would give a shout and blow a shofar to let her know to be ready. When the wedding party arrived at father's house, the newlyweds went into the wedding chamber for a seven-day honeymoon, and the groom's best friend stood outside waiting for the groom to tell him that the marriage had been consummated. Then all the friends really started celebrating for the seven days that the couple was honeymooning. When the couple emerged, there would be much congratulation and the marriage supper could begin.

Jesus understood the marriage customs in those days and compared it to how it will be when He comes for those who love Him. He compares the union of marriage among people the same as our union with Him. Jesus explains in Matthew 25:1–13 (RSV) the parable of the ten bridesmaids.

> Then the kingdom of heaven shall be compared to ten maidens who took their lamps and went to meet the bridegroom. Five of them were foolish, and five were wise. For when the foolish took their lamps, they took no oil with them; but the wise took flasks of oil with their

lamps. As the bridegroom was delayed, they all slumbered and slept. But at midnight there was a cry, "Behold, the bridegroom! Come out to meet him." Then all those maidens rose and trimmed their lamps. And the foolish said to the wise, "Give us some of your oil, for our lamps are going out." But the wise replied, "Perhaps there will not be enough for us and for you; go rather to the dealers and buy for yourselves." And while they went to buy, the bridegroom came, and those who were ready went in with him to the marriage feast; and the door was shut. Afterward the other maidens came also, saying "Lord, Lord open to us." But he replied, "Truly, I say to you, I do not know you." Watch therefore for you know neither the day nor the hour.

Jesus says there are many mansions in heaven. If there weren't, He would have told us. He went there to get places in heaven ready for us. And when He comes at His Second Coming, Jesus will take us back to heaven so we will always be with Him (John 14:2–3 NIV).

Be careful that you do not let your lamp oil run out. People get complacent in their Christian walk and lose their lamp oil. The bride of Christ, God's chosen people, are those who clothe themselves with righteous deeds. Your righteous deeds are symbolized by the lamp oil. As a follower of Christ, we cannot allow our light to go out because we have run out of oil—or rather righteous deeds. The marriage of the Lamb takes place immediately after the rapture, Christ's Second Coming. We are to clothe ourselves to be holy as God's chosen people, dressed with compassion, kindness, humility, gentleness, and patience. You need to forgive those you may have a grievance against. We expect the Lord to forgive us; likewise, we need to forgive others. But over all these virtues, put on love, which will bind them all together in perfect unity.

> Hallelujah! For the Lord our God the Almighty reigns. Let us rejoice and exult and give him the glory, for the marriage of the Lamb has come, and his Bride has made herself ready; it was granted her to be clothed with fine linen, bright and pure—for the fine linen is the righteous deeds of the saints. (Rev. 19:6–8 RSV)

God's angel said that we are blessed to be invited to the marriage supper of the Lamb. These are the true words of God. Then John tried to worship the angel by falling down at his feet. However, the angel stopped John and told him we must only worship God, for angels are servants just like us who hold the testimony of Jesus.

Three
SIGNS OF THE LORD'S SECOND COMING

In order to be watchful, it is crucial to understand and know the signs of the Lord's Second Coming. The Lord Himself gave us signs of His coming and throughout scriptures by the prophets. We are to be children of light, not darkness.

Now brothers, about times and dates we do not need to write to you, for you know very well that the day of the Lord will come like a thief in the night. While people are saying, "Peace and Safety," destruction will come on them suddenly, as labor pains on a pregnant woman, and they will not escape. But you, brothers, are not in darkness so that this day should surprise you like a thief. You are all sons of the light and sons of the day. We do not belong to the night or to the darkness. So then, let us not be like others, who are asleep, but let us be alert and self-controlled. (1 Thess. 5:1–6 NIV)

The various signs of the Lord's Second Coming have been revealed to us in many ways. This chapter explains only a few. The Lord uses the analogy of His coming like labor pains on a pregnant woman. This is because labor pains increase as time gets close to delivery. The same is true before Christ comes. The Lord told us that signs of His coming will increase as with the beginning of birth pains.

Jesus answered in Matthew 24:4–8 that people are going to experience many hardships and grieve over loved ones. People will die from plagues, earthquakes, and famines. Food will be hard to come by in most countries around the globe. Nations will be threatening war against each other. However, do not be afraid for God is with you. Do not believe in false gods proclaiming they are the Christ. Many will try to deceive you. But you know God's Word.

An alarming increase of earthquakes, wars, and fatal epidemic diseases (pestilences) are signs revealing that the time is drawing near to the Lord's coming and the birth of a new world. As time draws nearer, the signs of His coming increase in numbers and intensity. Today we are experiencing an increased number of earthquakes and storms.

Earthquake Statistics

The following are worldwide statistics showing the increase in the number of earthquakes there have been since year 1000:

Year	# Earthquakes
1000–1250	32
1251–1490	37
1491–1650	101
1651–1750	132
1751–1850	209
1851–1903	316
(Global)	
2000 (4.0M <)	9,513
2008 (4.0M <)	14,239

We are currently having a worldwide pandemic in which we are not done with it yet. Many countries have suffered through severe pandemics in the past, such as the black death, the bubonic plague, smallpox, cholera, Hong Kong flu, the Spanish flu, the Asian flu, HIV/AIDS, SARS, and now COVID-19. And I'm sure there will be other plagues the world will experience before the Lord comes.

The Lord has given us many signs to be watchful so we'll be ready for His Second Coming. Another sign that He is coming soon can be compared to a tree sprouting in the spring, letting us know that summer is near. When you see all these things, you know that the Lord will soon come. The generation that sees these things come to pass will see the coming of Christ Himself. God's words will never pass away.

The generation that sees Israel get their land back will be the generation to see His second return. We are that generation who saw Israel get their land back on May 14, 1948!

The Declaration of the Establishment of the State of Israel (May 14, 1948)

On May 14, 1948, on the day in which the British Mandate over a Palestine expired, the Jewish People's Council gathered at the Tel Aviv Museum and approved the following proclamation, declaring the establishment of the State of Israel. Israel's proclamation of independence was declared by the United Nations in May 1948; this established the first Jewish state in 2,000 years. The new state was recognized that night by the United States and three days later by the USSR.

The Lord says He will return when men are not able to rule themselves. When God decides men are not capable of ruling their kingdoms fairly and in peace, He will come down with His kingdom to rule the earth. Daniel 2 tells us that Jesus will return during the reign of the *Holy Roman Empire*. We are living in the reign of the Holy Roman Empire! It is essential to understand this prophecy by Daniel because we learn that the Antichrist and false prophet both come out of the Holy Roman Empire.

Daniel was a spiritual leader for King Nebuchadnezzar during the Babylonian Empire. During this time, King Nebuchadnezzar had a dream one night but woke up and could not remember it. It bothered him because he wanted to remember it and understand what it meant. So the king asked for his spiritual leaders to tell him what he dreamed and what it meant. Daniel was the only one who was able to explain what the king saw, including what the parts of the statue meant and the images symbolizing world empires. Only Daniel had an answer for the king. Daniel told the king in Daniel 2:27–45 (LB) that only God in heaven can reveal secrets. No astrologer, magician, wizard, or wise man is able to reveal secrets. But God told Daniel in his dream of future events to show this king for his benefit.

Daniel told the king about a horrifying shiny statue of a man who was extremely large and powerful. This statue had a head made of pure gold, its chest and arms were of silver, its belly and thighs were of brass, its legs were of iron, and its feet were part iron and part clay. However, Daniel saw that a rock was cut from the mountainside by supernatural means. This rock came hurling toward the statue and crushed to bits the feet of iron and clay. Then the whole statue collapsed into a heap of iron, clay, brass, silver, and gold; its pieces were crushed as small chaff, and the wind blew them all away. But the rock that knocked the statue down became a great mountain that covered the whole earth.

Now for the meaning of Daniel's dream, he explained to this king that God of heaven has given you your kingdom with power and strength and to rule over many kings. God decreed for you to rule the farthest provinces, and even the animals and birds are under your control. You are that head of gold. However, when your kingdom comes to an end, another world power will arise to take your place. This empire will be inferior to yours. When that empire falls, another third great power will come to rule the world, which is represented by the bronze belly of the statute. After that, the fourth kingdom will be strong as iron smashing, bruising, and conquering. The feet and toes you saw, part iron and part clay, show that later on this kingdom will be divided. Some parts of it will be as strong as iron and some as weak as clay. This mixture of iron with clay also show that these kingdoms will try to strengthen themselves by forming alliances with each other through intermarriage of their ruler, but this will not succeed for iron and clay don't mix.

While these kings are in power, the God of heaven will set up a kingdom that will never be destroyed; no one will ever conquer it. It will shatter all these kingdoms into nothingness, but it shall stand forever, indestructible. This explains the meaning of the rock cut from the mountain by supernatural means—the rock crushed to powder all the iron and brass, the clay, the silver, and the gold. Therefore, God has shown us what is going to happen and has given interpretation of your dream.

- head of gold—Babylonian Empire (606 BC–539 BC)
- chest and arms of silver—Medio/Persia Empire (536 BC–331 BC)
- belly and thighs of brass—Greek Empire (330 BC–197 BC)
- legs of iron—Roman Empire (197 BC–AD 284)
- feet mingled with iron and clay—Holy Roman Empire (AD 800)

Jesus Christ *is* that Rock spoken of in Daniel's dream. When Christ comes at His Second Coming, His kingdom here on earth will never be destroyed; Christ Himself will rule as King. But before the Lord comes, world order must be in place to fulfill the one world government that will be controlled by the beast, also known as the Antichrist. The new world order started with the formation of the North Atlantic Treaty Organization (NATO). The beast will rule over the one world government, and the mark of the beast (666) will be used to control and uphold the one world government. If you want to live with Christ, you must *not* take the mark of the beast. Although you might lose your life by not receiving the mark of the beast, you won't lose your eternal life and salvation. Anyone who submits to the beast and receives his mark will die, be condemned, and perish forever.

> He also forced everyone, small and great, rich
> and poor, free and slave, to receive a mark on

his right hand or on his forehead, so that no one could buy or sell unless he has the mark, which is the name of the beast, for it is a man's number. This calls for wisdom. If anyone has insight, let him calculate the number of the beast, or the number of his name, for it is a man's number of his name. His number is 666. (Rev. 13:16–18 NIV)

If you do not take the mark of the beast, you will not be able to work, possibly not receive medical attention, purchase a home, or buy food. The purpose of mandating this mark is to control you. The government will want to control everything you do. This mark of the beast will be a microchip that will be able to know everything about you. People will be living under a communist government. You will lose your freedom. However, I believe this will be for a short period of time. People who know their God, Jesus Christ, will need to abstain from receiving this deadly mark. If taken, it will lead to your death in this life and the life hereafter. Be strong in your faith and prepare. God is with you and always will be.

The Roman Empire was ruled by a worldly government with an emperor or king only. The Holy Roman Empire started in year 800, which had two rulers: either an emperor or king symbolized by iron *and* a religious emperor symbolized by clay. Pope Leo III announced on December 25, 800, that Pope Charlemagne was the new emperor, which changed the monarchy to *Holy* Roman Empire, now ruled by the king and pope. The Holy Roman Empire continued for the next one thousand plus years.

The Second Coming of our Lord will take place during the time of the *rebirth* of the Holy Roman Empire. After World War II, Europe was reduced to rubble; it had no economic or political power. The two superpowers were the Soviet Union and the United States of America. Winston Churchill knew that there had to be a radical change in Europe if they were to play a central role in world affairs or the Soviet Union and the United States would remain as the superpowers. So Churchill suggested establishing a "United States of Europe," having nations unify as one in Europe.

The Treaty of Rome created a Common Market and was signed in 1957, in which six nations joined. The first goal was to create an economic union, and then a political union would follow. All economic barriers were gone by 1992, and there were twelve members now of the Common Market. By 1999, twenty-five nations joined the Common Market and adopted the same money—the euro. By 2007, there were twenty-seven members who now belonged to the European Union; they were no longer called the Common Market. The European Union was now the world's number one economic power. But their mission was still not completed. The European Union is the prophesied "rebirth" of the Holy Roman Empire in which the Antichrist and false prophet will arise. The European Union printed up new money. Their first coin was printed with a picture of Emperor Charlemagne on it. Pope Charlemagne was crowned emperor when the Holy Roman Empire began in AD 800.

The European Union gives a "prize" every year to the one who did the most for the union. The prize is a gold medal that hangs around the neck (as the medal given to winners at the Olympics). The prize medal given has a picture of Emperor Charlemagne on it, and it is called the Charlemagne Prize. In 2000, US President Bill Clinton was given the prize for assisting with bringing Yugoslavia into the US of Europe. He was given the Charlemagne Prize in the cathedral at the coronation in Aachen, Germany, which was the home of Charlemagne. In 1987, Henry Kissinger was also given the Charlemagne Prize, as was General George C. Marshall in 1957.

The most influential magazine in Europe, *The Economist,* comes out weekly for kings and presidents. This magazine devotes one page to communicate the progress of the European unification. This special page is called the "Charlemagne Page."

Many nations are still applying to belong and become members of the European Union. To apply, they must send their applications to a place in Brussels, Belgium. The place they apply to is the Charlemagne Building.

This new nation, the European Union, must have a flag to represent itself. The flag was made with twelve stars in a circle. The stars were supposed to represent the number of nations, yet the union has twenty-seven members. The twelve stars were kept on the flag due to the twelve stars circling the head of the Virgin Mary; the European Union is led by the Catholic Church who represents the Virgin Mary. In addition, all vehicle license plates and money have the circle of twelve stars on them.

A great and wondrous sign appeared in heaven; a woman clothed with the sun, with the moon under her feet and a crown of twelve stars on her head. She was pregnant and cried out in pain as she was about to give birth … She gave birth to a son, a male child, who will rule all the nations with an iron scepter. (Rev. 12:1, 2, 5 NIV)

On October 29, 2004, the European Union adopted a constitution that was signed in the same place the Treaty of Rome was signed in 1957. All twenty-five nations had to agree on the constitution, except for the French and Dutch. They decided to convert the constitution to a new treaty.

Therefore, in Lisbon, Portugal, all twenty-seven nations became one on December 13, 2007, and signed. The last nation to ratify the treaty was the Czech Republic. When they did, the Treaty of the Constitution of the European Union was completed on November 3, 2009. The Second Coming of our Lord Jesus Christ will come when the European Union will be in power, which is also the Holy Roman Empire.

Revelations 17 explains about a beast having seven heads and ten horns, with a woman (symbol of the Vatican) sitting on this world government. This is the power of the Antichrist—power of politics and religion. The Antichrist comes out of the iron mingled with clay. The Antichrist and false prophet rule together.

The most significant sign you need to watch for is the signing of a seven-year peace agreement (treaty) with Israel and Palestine.

The confirmation of this Seven Year covenant will:

- Confirm Israel's right to the land, which currently is denied by Israel's enemies (Gen. 15:18).
- The borders of Israel will be established.
- The Temple Mount will be placed under a sharing arrangement under international authority.
- And will allow the building of Israel's third temple—preparations are already made. (Endtime, 2016)

President Donald Trump had a peace treaty drawn up and completed in spring 2020, between Israel and of few of her enemies, yet it was not signed by Palestine. President Trump had gotten nations to accept and sign the agreement in summer 2020. This treaty included all the components stated above and more. This peace treaty is acceptable to Israel and was hopeful to be accepted by Israel's surrounding enemies (nations). However, when this seven-year peace agreement is signed, it will be in deceit and will be broken by Israel's enemies forty-two months (three and a half years) later. Before the covenant is broken, Israel will begin performing their sacrifices in their new temple. When the covenant is broken, the Antichrist will be revealed, he sets himself up in the holy place (God's temple), and he calls himself god. This specific act is referred to the *abomination of desolation.* The Antichrist will stop Israel from performing sacrifices because he is now claiming to be god, and he will refuse to allow anyone to worship the God of Abraham. The Antichrist will demand all to worship him. The great tribulation and the mark of the beast begins. Daniel 9:27 (LB) says the Antichrist, king, is going to confirm the seven-year covenant with Israel. Yet after three and a half years, he will break this treaty and stop the Jews from performing their sacrifices and offerings. Then to top off all these terrible deeds, the enemy shall completely defile God's sanctuary. But in God's time and plan, his judgment will be poured out upon this evil one.

So, when you see the desolation sacrilege spoken of by the prophet Daniel, standing in the holy place (let the reader understand), then let those who are in Judea flee to the mountains; let him who is on the housetop not go down to take what is in his house; and let him who is in the field not turn back to take his mantle. And alas, for those who are with child and for those who give suck in those days! Pray that your flight may not be in winter or on a Sabbath. For then there will be great tribulation, such as has not been from the beginning of the world until now, no, and never will be. (Matt. 24:15–21 RSV)

In the Old Testament, people had to perform sacrifices to be forgiven of their sins. However, in the New Testament, Jesus Christ was born and the Law was observed differently but not abolished. God still expects us to abide by the Ten Commandments. However, if we believe in Jesus Christ as the Son of God who died for our sins, then we are forgiven without performing sacrifices by killing a lamb, goat, or calf. This is because Christ replaced the sacrifices that were performed throughout the ages of the Old Testament for the sins of the people. Christ was the sacrificial Lamb who replaced the old tradition of sacrificing for your sins when He shed His blood and died on the cross. Jesus said in Matthew 5:17 (NIV), "Do not think that I have come to abolish the Law or the Prophets; I have not come to abolish them but to fulfill them."

Another law that is held in reverence by God, along with the Ten Commandments, is in reference to the seven feasts that were followed strictly in the Old Testament. The Old Testament law had the Jews perform sacrifices with animals for these seven Holy Feasts, which was the law. Four of these feasts have already been fulfilled by Christ. Additionally, Christ will fulfill the other three when He comes again. This means sacrifices will not be performed for these holy feasts because Jesus Christ was the sacrifice. Leviticus 23:2 (NIV) describes the seven feasts in order of their seasonal observance. "These are my appointed feasts, the appointed feasts of the Lord, which you are to proclaim as sacred assemblies."

1. Feast of Passover: spring (fulfilled by Christ—crucifixion)

   We are redeemed and set free by the blood of Jesus, the Passover Lamb of God.

2. Feast of Unleavened Bread: spring (fulfilled by Christ–sanctification)

   This feast begins the day after the Passover Eve and lasts for seven days. Leaven in scripture is usually a symbol of sin; the matzo graphically portrays the pure and sinless Messiah.

3. Feast of Firstfruits: spring (fulfilled by Christ–Resurrection)

   Celebrated the day after the Feast of Unleavened Bread. It is a holiday giving thanks for the barley harvest, the first grain of the season. Jesus is the Firstfruit whom God raised from the dead.

4. Feast of Weeks (Pentecost): late spring (fulfilled by Christ–coming of the Holy Spirit)

   It comes fifty days after the Passover; thus, the Greek name Pentecost, which means "fifty."

5. Feast of Trumpets: early autumn (not fulfilled)

   Commonly known as Rosh Hashanah, this marks the beginning of the civil year and is the Jewish New Year's Day. In Leviticus 23:24, God commanded the blowing of trumpets on the first day of the seventh month to call the congregation of Israel together for a very solemn assembly.

6. Day of Atonement: autumn (not fulfilled) (Yom Kippur)

The Jews fast and pray in solemn assembly for repentance and forgiveness under the Law. The believers in Christ are forgiven by one atonement for all time. The rest of Israel will repent and look to its Messiah one day.

7. Feast of Tabernacles: autumn (final harvest) (not fulfilled)

   Also known as Feast of Booths or Ingathering. Known in Hebrew as Succoth. This is the final fall harvest festival, a time of ingathering at Jerusalem. It is the harvest celebration and memorial of tabernacles in the wilderness. Booths speak of the final rest, as well as the final harvest. John wrote in Revelation 21:3 (NKJ), "Behold, the tabernacle of God is with men, and He will dwell with them, and they shall be His people, and God Himself will be with them and be their God."

End of the Age Outline

Many people believe the seals, trumpets, and vials in the book of Revelation are on a sequential timeline, but they are not. The seals are on a timeline separate from the trumpets, and in some cases they coincide together. However, the vials do start after Christ calls, with the sound of the *last* trumpet for the saints to come up, which is the rapture. The vials are God's wrath on those who were not raptured at Christ's Second Coming; they were not invited to the marriage supper with the Lamb.

1st Seal – White horse represents *Catholicism*; began years ago.	**1st Trumpet** – 1914, WWI: 1/3 of earth set on fire, 1/3 of trees and grass burned.
2nd Seal – Red horse represents *communism;* began years ago.	**2nd Trumpet** – 1939, WWII: 1/3 of ships destroyed, 1/3 of water became blood.
3rd Seal – Black horse represents *capitalism;* inflation and cost of living rises.	**3rd Trumpet** – 1986, Wormwood, Chernobyl incident.
4th Seal – Pale horse represents Islamism; peace agreement is signed (the final seven years).	**4th Trumpet** – In 1989, it was noted that time and speed are now related to each other creating days to be shorter.
5th Seal – The great tribulation; WWIII begins at Euphrates River.	**5th Trumpet** – 1990, Saddam Hussein (Apollyon) burned oil wells; skies blackened, no sun.

6th **Seal** – End of great tribulation; Rapture of God's people takes place.	6th **Trumpet** – Final seven years begin; Jewish temple rebuilt, sacrifices begin, WWIII peace broken, 1/3 of humankind dies; Antichrist stops sacrifices, great tribulation begins.
7th **Seal** – The golden censer.	7th **Trumpet** – Rapture of God's people! Marriage supper begins!

The sound of the trumpet is used many times throughout scriptures. There is significant meaning for the Lord to use the trumpet call for specific reasons, which is why the shofar is blown. The shofar will be blown for the world to hear when our Lord Jesus Christ calls for His faithful followers at the rapture.

The word *shofar* is not found in our English translations of the scriptures but is translated ram's horn, coronet, or trumpet. It is mentioned over eighty times in the scriptures. There are two types of instruments in the scriptures that are called trumpets. One is the shofar, a ram's horn, or a Yemenite horn, a silver trumpet. The shofar was most often a horn from a male sheep but could have been from any animal if it was "kosher," the exception being a cow or a steer, due to the golden calf incident. The longer twisted horn is called a Yemenite horn and comes from an African antelope called kudu.

The blowing of the trumpet will be called on the tenth day of the seventh month for the jubilee celebration. And on the Day of Atonement, the shofar will be heard throughout the land (Lev. 25:9–10 NKJV).

The following are some of the major scriptures describing the use of the shofar:

- The Torah was given to Israel with the sound of the shofar (Ex. 19:19).
- The shofar was blown to announce the beginning of festivals (Num. 10:10).
- The shofar was blown to signal the assembly of the Israelites during war (Jud. 3:27).
- The shofar was blown for the coronation of a king (1 Kings 1:34–39).
- The shofar is a reminder that Yahweh is sovereign (Ps. 47:5).
- The shofar was blown to celebrate the new moon on Rosh Hashanah (Ps. 81:1–3).
- The shofar will be blown at the time of the ingathering of the exiles of Israel to their place (Isa. 27:13).

- The blowing of the shofar ushers in the Day of Adonai (Joel 2:1).
- The shofar will be blown at the Resurrection of the dead (1 Thess. 4:16).

Four
THE SEALS

⸻∞⸻

The four horsemen spoken of in the seals of the book of Revelation are spirits.

The first chariot had red horses, the second black, the third white, and the fourth dappled—all of them powerful. I asked the angel who was speaking to me, "What are these, my lord?" The angel answered me, "These are the four spirits of heaven, going out from standing in the presence of the Lord of the whole world. The one with the black horses is going toward the north country, the one with the white horse toward the west, and the one with the dappled horses toward the south." (Zech. 6:2–6 NIV)

First Seal

The first horseman is riding a white horse, which represents Catholicism.

> I watched as the Lamb opened the first of the seven seals. Then I heard one of the four living creatures say in a voice like thunder "Come!" I looked, and there before me was a white horse! Its rider held a bow, and was given a crown, and he rode out as a conqueror bent on conquest. (Rev. 6:1–2 NIV)

The pope usually wears a white robe, rides a white vehicle, and wears a crown on his head. The *Roman Catholic Church* has a history that reaches back 2,000 years and touches all corners of the globe. That said, it has not been without its share of both internal and external conflict. The Roman Catholic Church is the world's largest religious denomination, with 1.2 billion believers worldwide. This number makes it only slightly smaller than Islam (1.4 billion) and larger than any other religious group on the planet. From its spiritual center in Vatican City, the world's smallest independent country and the only country surrounded completely by a city (Rome), the leader of the Catholic Church, Pope Francis I, guides the spiritual lives of whole countries. By definition, the word *catholic* means "universal," and from the earliest days following the church's founding, it has pressed to be the universal faith of humanity. Often this means severe conflicts with others who wish to be the universal faith, both within and outside of the Christian tradition (Newton, 2003).

Second Seal

The second horseman is riding a red horse, which represents communism.

> When the Lamb opened the second seal, I heard the second living creature say, "Come!" Then another horse came out, a fiery red one. Its rider was given power to take peace from the earth and to make men slay each other. To him was given a large sword. (Rev. 6:3–4 NIV)

For many years, the term *red* was synonymous with communism. The color continues to be used in the flags and symbolism of communist countries such as China and Vietnam. The color red has been used to symbolize rebellion for centuries and came to be identified with left-wing political movements dating from the eighteenth century. The most common reason given by communists for using red is that it symbolizes the blood of the proletariat, or working class, which was shed in their revolution (Markey, 2001).

Third Seal

The third horseman is riding a black horse, which represents capitalism, inflation, and cost of living rises.

When the Lamb opened the third seal, I heard the third living creature say, "Come!" I looked, and there before me was a black horse! Its rider was holding a pair of scales in his hand. Then I heard what sounded like a voice among the four living creatures, saying, "A quart of wheat for a day's wages, and three quarts of barley for a day's wages, and do not damage the oil and the wine." (Rev. 6:5–6 NIV)

During this period, the world will be experiencing the high cost of living. The price of food will go up tremendously due to scarcity. Gasoline for vehicles and heating our homes will be extremely high as well. And the cost of general goods and basic supplies will also be high due to lack of availability for various reasons. Some countries have cost of living expenditures set by their own government, and other countries are run by capitalism.

Capitalism is a free-market economy that creates inflation due to not being regulated by the government. Capitalism is an economic system based on private ownership of the means of production and the creation of goods and services for profit. Central characteristics of capitalism include private property, capital accumulation, wage labor, and competitive markets. In a capitalist market economy, investments are determined by private decision and the parties to a transaction typically determine the prices at which they exchange assets, goods, and services (Wikipedia).

During this time, we will be dealing with extreme weather changes and plagues that are bound to influence our food chain and supplies.

Fourth Seal

The fourth horseman is riding a pale horse, which represents Islamism.

> When the Lamb opened the fourth seal, I heard the voice of the fourth living creature say, "Come!" I looked, and there before me was a pale horse! Its rider was named Death, and Hades was following close behind him. They were given power over a fourth of the earth to kill by sword, famine and plague, and by the wild beasts of the earth. (Rev. 6:7–8 NIV)

The rider on the pale horse represents death. The color "pale" was translated for the word *chloros* (green) from the original scriptures because it did not make common sense to call the horse chloros or green. Mark 6:39 references to the green grass, including Revelation 9:4. Islam's national color is green. The wrought iron around the Temple Mount is green. The gates, Islam's flag, and doors on the mosque are green. Rider on the green horse is death. Islam glorifies death. The green horseman will have power over the fourth part of the earth; 1.3–1.8 billion people on earth are Muslims. Ninety-six percent of Muslims are from Africa and South Asia and are in poverty, dying of hunger.

Iran and other nations will cause great trouble for Israel and surrounding countries. They will threaten Israel with a nuclear hit, but the United States will intervene. The United States has always protected Israel. The ruler over America will go after Iran with great power.

Now besides war and hunger being the cause of death, another cause is plague. In these end times, it is possible that this plague is a bioweapon. A bioweapon can be a bacterium, virus, vaccine, or several other organisms used with the intent to kill, harm, or incapacitate humans, animals, or plants.

Fifth Seal

The great tribulation begins.

> When he opened the fifth seal, I saw under the altar the souls of those who had been slain because of the word of God and the testimony they had maintained. They called out in a loud voice, "How long, Sovereign Lord, holy and true, until you judge the inhabitants of the earth and avenge our blood?" Then each of them was given a white robe, and they were told to wait a little longer, until the number of their fellow servants and brother who were to

be killed as they had been was completed. (Rev. 6:9–11 NIV)

Approximately 2.3 billion will be killed during the great tribulation. In Revelation 9:13–18, the sixth trumpet talks about a war that kills one-third of the human race from the Euphrates River, which is controlled by Islam.

Sixth Seal

The Second Coming of our Lord Jesus Christ takes place on the Sixth Seal, after the great tribulation. Five major events are described. Jesus told us the following:

1. Sun will be darkened.
2. Moon shall not give her light.
3. Stars fall from heaven.
4. The powers of the heavens will be shaken.
5. Then shall appear the sign of the coming of the Son of man.

Immediately after the tribulation of those days the sun will be darkened, and the moon will not give its light, and the stars will fall from heaven, and the powers of the heavens will be shaken; then will appear the sign of the Son of man in heaven, and then all the tribes of the earth will mourn, and they will see the Son of man coming on the clouds of heaven with power and great glory; and will send out his angels with a loud trumpet call, and they will gather his elect from the four winds, from one end of heaven to the other. (Matt. 24:29–31 RSV)

For the Lord himself will come down from heaven, with a loud command, with the voice of the archangel and with the trumpet call of God, and the dead in Christ will rise first. After that, we who are still alive and are left will be caught up with them in the clouds to meet the Lord in the air. And so, we will be with the Lord forever. (1 Thess. 4:16–17 NIV)

Revelation 6:12–16 describes the same as follows:

- great earthquake
- sun black as sackcloth of hair
- moon became as blood
- stars fallen from heaven
- Second Coming of Christ

When he opened the sixth seal, I looked, and behold, there was a great earthquake; and the sun became black as sackcloth, the full moon became like blood, and the stars of the sky fell to the earth as the fig tree sheds its winter fruit when shaken by a gale; the sky vanished like a scroll that is rolled up, and every mountain and island was removed from its place. Then the kings of the earth and the great men and the generals and the rich and the strong, and every one, slave and free, hid in the caves and among the rocks of the mountains, calling to the mountains and rocks, "Fall on us and hide us from the face of him who is seated on the throne, and from the wrath of the Lamb; for the great day of their wrath has come, and who can stand before it." (Rev. 6:12–17 RSV)

The sixth seal coincides with the seventh trumpet.

Seventh Seal

When the lamb had broken the seventh seal, there was silence throughout all heaven for what seemed like half an hour ... Then the angel filled the censer with fire from the altar and threw it down upon the earth; and thunder crashed and rumbled, lightning flashed, and there was a terrible earthquake. (Rev. 8:1, 3 LB)

Five
THE TRUMPETS

First Trumpet

One-third of the earth was set on fire, and one-third of the trees and grass was burned. This happened in 1914 during World War I when 9 million died; 1.7 billion was the population. "The first angel sounded his trumpet, and there came hail and fire mixed with blood, and it was hurled down upon the earth. A third of the earth was burned up, a third of the trees were burned up, and all the green grass was burned up" (Rev. 8:7 NIV). The battles fought during World War I were mostly ground battles. They were fought with stationary cannons, men on horseback using swords and guns, moving tanks with cannons, and bombs from airplanes. Men dug miles of trenches to take refuge. Massive trees and grass were burned up. Most visible were dirt and smoke from the cannons, bombs, and gunfire.

Second Trumpet

One-third of ships in the sea were destroyed and one-third of the waters in the sea became blood. This happened in 1939, during World War II when over 50 million died; 2.3 billion was the population.

> The second angel sounded his trumpet, and something like a huge mountain, all ablaze, was thrown into the sea. A third of the sea turned into blood, a third of the living creatures in the sea dies, and a third of the ships were destroyed. (Rev. 8:8–9 NIV)

World War II was a global war that lasted from 1939 to 1945. It was the most widespread war in history and directly involved more than 100 million people from over thirty countries. Marked by mass deaths of civilians, including the Holocaust (in which approximately 11 million people were killed) and the strategic bombing of industrial and population centers (in which 1 million were killed and which included the atomic bombings of Hiroshima and Nagasaki), it resulted in an estimated 50 million to 85 million fatalities. These made World War II the deadliest conflict in human history (Wikipedia).

Third Trumpet

Great burning star fell: Wormwood. In 1986, the Chernobyl disaster happened.

> The third angel sounded his trumpet, and a great star, blazing like a torch, fell from the sky on a third of the rivers and on the springs of water—the name of the star is Wormwood. A third of the waters turned bitter, and many people died from the waters that had become bitter. (Rev. 8:10–11 NIV)

The disaster occurred on April 26, 1986, in Ukraine, then part of the Soviet Union. Many innocent people died that day. More died in the ensuing weeks. And millions—yes, millions—more will be laid to rest long before their natural time, their bones helplessly infected with the radioactive material cesium-137.

The Chernobyl Disaster, a secular book by Soviet-born Viktor Haynes, begins not with an introduction but with the prophecy and a quote from *The Concise Oxford Dictionary,* sixth edition. "Chernobyl is a Russian transliteration of the Ukrainian word *chernoby,* which in English means wormwood, 'a perennial herb of genus Artemisia with bitter, tonic, and stimulation qualities used in preparation of vermouth, absinthe and in medicine.'" According to the *Dictionary of the Russian Language* by S. Ozhegov, the word *chernobylnik* means "a variety of absinthe (wormwood) wither-brown or deep purple stem." The book *Chernobyl: A Documentary Story* by Iurii Sheherbak, translated from the Ukrainian language, says "Ancient Chernobyl" gave its bitter name (Chernobyl is the common wormwood) to the powerful nuclear power station whose construction began in 1971 (Endtime, 2001).

Fourth Trumpet

This tells of the shortening of days, not number of days. "The fourth angel sounded his trumpet, and a third of the sun was struck, a third of the moon, and a third of the stars, so that a third of them turned dark. A third of the day was without light, and a third of the night" (Rev. 8:12 NIV). In 1915, the theory of relativity was discovered by Albert Einstein, and time and speed were not relative to each other. Then in 1989, it was discovered that time and speed were now relative to each other, creating days to be shorter. During this same period, the Berlin Wall fell and the new world order began.

Fifth Trumpet

Kuwait oil fires, Persian Gulf War. In 1991, Saddam Hussein burned seven hundred oil wells. For months, the skies were blackened; no sun could be seen. Saddam means "destroyer." The name in Hebrew is Abaddon; in Greek, Apoloyn.

The fifth angel sounded his trumpet, and I saw a star that had fallen from the sky to the earth. The star was given the key to the shaft of the Abyss. When he opened the Abyss, smoke rose from it like the smoke from a gigantic furnace. The sun and sky were darkened by the smoke from the Abyss. And out of the smoke locusts came down upon the earth and were given power like that of the scorpions of the earth. They were told not to harm the grass of the earth or any plant or tree, but only those people who did not have the seal of God on their foreheads. They were not given power to kill them, but only to torture them for five months. And the agony they suffered was like that of the sting of a scorpion when it strikes a man. (Rev. 9:1–5 NIV)

When Iraqi troops withdrew from Kuwait at the end of the Persian Gulf War in early 1991, they set fire to more than six hundred oil wells and pools of spilled oil. The Kuwait oil fires burned for more than eight months, consuming an estimated 5 to 6 million barrels of crude oil and 70 to 100 million cubic meters of natural gas per day. The geography and climate of the Persian Gulf region affected the distribution of the oil well plumes as well as the severity of their effect on human populations and natural ecosystems. Uneven heating of the land and sea surfaces created local atmospheric inversions during the summer months that trapped smoke in the lower atmosphere and occasionally caused the plumes to blanket the Kuwaiti land surface. Violent sandstorms, driven by intense summer winds, mixed sand and dust with the smoke plumes (Duncan, 2004).

Sixth Trumpet

The final seven years begin with the signing of the seven-year peace agreement with Israel and Palestine. The Antichrist will confirm several peace agreements with Israel and neighboring countries. However, the peace agreement between Israel and Palestine is the covenant that begins the last seven-year period spoken of by Daniel the profit. The Jewish temple will be rebuilt, and animal sacrifices will begin.

After three and a half years, the peace agreement is broken and the abomination of desolation (Antichrist) sets himself up in the temple, claims to be God, and stops the animal sacrifices. World War III starts and one-third of humankind dies. War starts at the Euphrates River (which is 97 percent Islamic); 2.3 billion will die; the world population is 7 billion.

> The sixth angel blew his trumpet, and I heard a voice coming from the horns of the golden altar that is before God. It said to the sixth angel who had the trumpet, "Release the four angels who are bound at the great river Euphrates." And the four angels who had been kept ready for this very hour and day and month and year were released to kill a third of humankind. The number of the mounted troops was two hundred million, I heard their number. (Rev. 9:13–16 NIV)

During this period of time, the Lord is going to give power to two witnesses to tell of what is to come for 1,260 days. Anyone who tries to do harm to these prophets will be killed by bursts of fire shooting from their mouths. These two prophets will be given power by the Lord to close up the skies so that no rain will fall during these three and a half years they are called to prophesy. They will turn rivers and oceans to blood and send every kind of plague as often as they want upon the earth.

After the three and a half years that these two prophets have completed their testimony, Satan will declare war against them. Satan will defeat them, and for three and a half days, their bodies will lie in the streets of Jerusalem exposed for all to see. This just happens to be the very place where our Lord was crucified. No one will be allowed to bury them. People from many parts of the world will stand around to gaze at their dead bodies. Since people will be so excited about the death of these two prophets who brought so much torment upon them that they will create a worldwide holiday! People will rejoice and give presents to each other and throw parties to celebrate the death of these two prophets who were sent by God to give a message to the world.

> However, after the three and a half days, these two prophets have laid dead, God is going to put the spirit of life back into them and they will stand up! God will shout from heaven and call out for them to "Come up!" They will then rise to heaven in a cloud as their enemies watch with great fear. (Rev. 11:3–12 LB)

Seventh Trumpet

Takes place with the sixth seal. The rapture of the saints takes place at the *last* trumpet call.

> Lo, I tell you a mystery. We shall not all sleep, but we shall all be changed, in a moment, in the twinkling of an eye, **at the last trumpet**. For the trumpet will sound, and the dead will be raised imperishable, and we shall be change. (1 Cor. 15:51–52 RSV; emphasis mine).

> The seventh angel sounded his trumpet, and there were loud voices in heaven, which said: "The kingdom of the world has become the kingdom of our Lord and of his Christ, and He will reign forever and ever." And the twenty-four elders, who were seated on their thrones

before God, fell on their faces and worshiped God, saying:

"We give thanks to you, Lord God Almighty, who is and who was, because you have taken your great power and have begun to reign. The nations were angry; and your wrath has come. The time has come for judging the dead, and for rewarding your servants the prophets and your saints and those who reverence your name, both small and great—and for destroying those who destroy the earth." (Rev. 11:15–19 NIV)

Six
THE VIALS,
GOD'S WRATH

The vials are God's wrath on those that were not rapture at Christ's calling of believers; they were not invited to the marriage supper with the Lamb. Therefore, in order to avoid going through God's wrath, you must be taken out by the Lord's rapture. Life will be extremely challenging before the rapture, and for some it will be very difficult. The devil is working in many ways to distort the truth. He will be working his hardest to gain control over you through people, the media, and corporations. The devil knows his time is short and will soon come to an end. We are in a spiritual warfare between good and evil. Do not let your guard down and be complacent. Do not unite or be a part of the one world government who will promote and enforce a one world religion. Do not be a part of the one world religion no matter how good they make it sound. Keep your eyes, ears, and heart focused on the God of Abraham, Isaac, and Jacob—our Lord Jesus Christ.

Second Peter 1:1–12 tells us to obtain

- knowledge of God
- diligence—faith virtue, virtue of knowledge
- knowledge to self-control
- self-control to perseverance
- perseverance of godliness

Then I looked, and lo, a white cloud and seated on the cloud one like a son of man, with a golden crown on his head, and a sharp sickle in his hand. And another angel came out the temple, calling with a loud voice to him who sat upon the cloud, "Put in your sickle, and reap, for the hour to reap has come; for the harvest of the earth is fully ripe." So, he who sat upon the cloud swung his sickle on the earth, and the earth was reaped. And another angel came out of the temple in heaven, and he too had a sharp sickle. Then another angel came out from the altar, the angel who has power over fire, and he called with a loud voice to him who had the sharp sickle; "Put in your sickle and gather the clusters of the vine of the earth, for its grapes are ripe." So the angel swung his sickle on the earth and gathered the vintage of the earth, and threw it into the great wine press of the wrath of God: and the wine press was trodden outside the city, and blood flowed from the wine press, as high as a horse's bridle, for one thousand six hundred stadia (Which is about two hundred miles). (Rev. 14:14–16 RSV)

"Then I heard a loud voice from the temple saying to the seven angels, 'Go pour out the seven vials of God's wrath on the earth'" (Rev. 16:1 NIV).

(Some Bibles use the term *vial;* some use the term *bowl.*)

First Vial

"The first angel went and poured out his bowl on the land, and ugly and painful sores broke out on the people who had the mark of the beast and worshipped his image" (Rev. 16:2 NIV). When people receive the mark of the beast and worship his image, they will experience horrible painful sores on their body. This might be due to a bad chemical used to insert the chip, from a plague, or possibly just due to God's punishment for not obeying Him. The mark of the beast or worshipping the image of the beast is and has been described by many people in different ways. Most people believe that a chip implanted in your hand or forehead is the mark of the beast. This is because a chip can reveal so much of your personal identification. This chip will identify you, provide your address, personal bank information, and have the ability to do much more. The Lord does not want you to have this chip because it is Satan's way of controlling you. The chip is how our government, who will be ruled by the beast, will know everything about you and probably be able to manipulate you through its technology unknown to us.

Inclusively, God wants you to pray, worship, and count on Him through these extremely difficult times. Remember you will not be able to purchase food or any goods during the three and a half years of the great tribulation that are before the rapture and through God's wrath (the vials) without the mark. It is unknown what the period of time is during God's wrath, although it is probably several days. Christ will return and fulfill the Feast of Trumpets beginning with the rapture, then bring those from His wrath for judgment by the Day of Atonement.

God wants you to rely on Him to make it through before He comes for us at His Second Coming, which starts with the rapture of His elect. Then those who do not make the rapture and have to endure His wrath can still be redeemed by worshipping only our Lord and Savior Christ Jesus. Never give in to the beast!

Second Vial

"The second angel poured out his bowl on the sea, and it turned into blood like that of a dead man, and every living thing in the sea died" (Rev. 16:3 NIV). Is it possible that the sea turns into blood after flowing from the wine press? After all, blood will reach as high as a horse's head and flow for two hundred miles!

The Nile River was turned to blood after Moses had ordered Pharaoh to release the Israelites from Egypt and he refused to do so. This massive river that turned to blood was one of the ten plagues Egypt encountered due to Pharaoh not obeying God. The people counted on the Nile for their drinking water and fish to eat.

Third Vial

The third angel poured out his bowl on the rivers and springs of water, and they became blood.

> Then I heard the angel in charge of the waters say: You are just in these judgments, you who are and who were, the Holy One, because you have so judged; for they have shed the blood of your saints and prophets, and you have given them blood to drink as they deserve. And I heard the altar respond: Yes, Lord God Almighty, true and just are your judgments. (Rev. 16:4–7 NIV)

Fourth Vial

> The fourth angel poured out his bowl on the
> sun, and the sun was given power to scorch
> people with fire. They were seared by the
> intense heat, and they cursed the name of
> God, who had control over these plagues, but
> they refused to repent and glorify him. (Rev.
> 16:8–9 NIV)

Other than a nuclear war causing the intense heat, it
could be from technology that can control our weather.
This technology is called HAARP (High Frequency Active
Auroral Research Program). HAARP was operated and
funded in 1993 by the US Air Force, US Navy, and other
entities. I believe in the past years it has been used for reasons
other than it was designed for, such as to manipulate and
control people. HAARP can do great harm by creating severe
flooding, hurricanes/tornadoes, earthquakes, and extreme
heat. Although the main HAARP station is near Gakona,
Alaska, there are numerous HAARP stations throughout
the world. The purpose for the creation of HAARP was
to study the science of the ionosphere and to understand
and enhance communications and surveillance systems
for civilians and defense. It also creates a very large radio
frequency to transmit electromagnetic beams into the
ionosphere or atmosphere. The severe weather conditions
that we have been experiencing have been controlled by
evil elite hierarchy to cause harm to people and to rule the

earth. They are getting ready for the great battle with our Lord Jesus Christ at His Second Coming. God might be the one causing the heat, or He is allowing this to happen by man for His purpose.

So instead of people humbling themselves before God and worshipping the God of all creation, they will curse Him. They will act like children being punished for their wrongdoing. If you don't make the rapture, you can make it through God's wrath if you repent and pray intensely. For the Lord your God will help you through these plagues.

Fifth Vial

> The fifth angel poured out his bowl on the throne of the beast, and his kingdom was plunged into darkness. Men gnawed their tongues in agony and cursed the God of heaven because of their pains and their sores, but they refused to repent of what they had done. (Rev. 16:10–11 NIV)

The Antichrist (beast) and his kingdom will be gone. No one will be able to worship the beast. Too many will die through God's wrath, and those who are left will wish they would have died and be disabled due to their crippling pains and sores.

Sixth Vial

> The sixth angel poured out his bowl on the great river Euphrates, and its water was dried up to prepare the way for the kings from the East. Then I saw three evil spirits that looked like frogs; they came out of the mouth of the dragon, out of the mouth of the beast and out of the mouth of the false prophet. They are spirits of demons performing miraculous signs, and they go out to the kings of the whole world, to gather them for the battle on the great day of God Almighty. Behold, I come like a thief! Blessed is he who stays awake and keeps his clothes with him, so that he may not go naked and be shamefully exposed. Then they gathered the kings together to the place that in Hebrew is called Armageddon. (Rev. 16:12–16 NIV)

The Euphrates River will dry up from no rain for three and a half years. Then there will be scorching heat from the plague administered in God's wrath. This was a part of God's plan to assist the nations from the east to the battlefield named Armageddon, which is near the city of Megiddo, Israel.

Seventh Vial

The seventh angel poured out his bowl into the air, and out of the temple came a loud voice from the throne, saying, "It is done!" Then there came flashes of lightning, rumblings, peals of thunder and a severe earthquake. No earthquake like it has ever occurred since man has been on earth, so tremendous was the quake. The great city split into three parts, and the cities of the nation's collapse. God remembered Babylon the Great and gave her the cup filled with the wine of the fury of his wrath. Every island fled away, and the mountains could not be found. From the sky huge hailstones of about a hundred pounds each fell upon men. And they cursed God on account of the plague of hail, because the plague was so terrible. (Rev. 16:17–21 NIV)

Seven

PREPARING FOR THE LORD'S COMING

———— ⌾⌾⌾ ————

To be prepared for the Lord's coming, you do not need to sell your house, quit your job, move out to the woods, and hide from what is to come. The Lord expects you to keep on living and look forward to your future and His coming. You need to be prepared to meet the Lord, whether it is at the rapture or you are taken before His coming. What God does expect of you is to love Him above all else. If you love someone, you want to know that person, please them, and have a relationship with them. In order to have a relationship with God, you need to know His Word—the Holy Bible.

In reading God's Word, you will learn about Him and how He wants you to live. God wants you to have patience, love, and endurance and live for what is good. God does not want you to be a lover of evil or worship anything other than Him. God sees what you do. Repent and change your ungodly ways to godliness. Don't be someone who says they believe in God yet does not show it. Many claim they believe but do not know God or live according to what God expects of them.

> I know your deeds, that you are neither cold nor hot. I wish you were either one or the other! So, because you are lukewarm—neither hot nor cold—I am about to spit you out of my mouth. (Rev. 3:15–16 NIV)

The only way you can know how to live according to God's will is to know God's Word. Therefore, get to know God by attending a church that teaches that Jesus Christ is the Son of God who died for your sins and was resurrected from the dead. If you are unable to attend church, then listen to church messages on television or radio broadcastings or read books that give understanding to biblical scriptures.

God expects us to be kind, respectful, and considerate toward everyone. If you are doing this and sharing the gospel with others, you are sowing good seeds. Jesus answered the disciples who wanted to understand the Lord's parable of the mustard seed. Jesus explained about good seeds and bad. The good seed appears to be dead until it falls on the ground, receives water, and grows into a tree. But bad seeds are weeds. Those who sow good seeds by sharing God's Word and being considerate and helpful to other people are the Son of Man. Hopefully what you share and how you treat others will inspire those to do the same. The field is the world, the good seeds are the sons of the kingdom, and the weeds are from the wicked one. The enemy who sows the bad seeds is the devil.

At the close of the age, God will command the angels to reap and harvest the bad seeds. Just like weeds are gathered and burned with fire, the same will be at the close of this age. God will send His angels out into the world to gather all causes of sin and all evildoers out of His kingdom and throw them into the furnace of fire; there men will be weeping and gnashing their teeth. Then the righteous will shine like the sun in the kingdom of their Father (Matt. 13:37–43 RSV).

Hard times are coming before the Lord comes for us. There will be three and a half years of great tribulation, which starts halfway through the seven-year peace covenant, then World War III breaks out. However, very soon thereafter, the Lord will come for us before He starts His wrath (vials) out upon the earth. The following is a list of things you should do and should not do to be ready:

Things You Should Do

1. Love God. There is only *one* God: the God of Abraham, Jacob, and Isaac.
2. Be born again. Be baptized with water and the Holy Spirit.

3. Know the *Truth*. There is one salvation; believe that Jesus is the Son of God, He died for your sins, and He was resurrected from the dead.

4. Stay with doctrines of the Bible. Satan will be trying his hardest to deceive you during these times and get you to believe in false doctrines.

5. Teach the Gospel and baptize. The Lord tells us to teach others the scriptures and baptize them.

6. Pray daily. Stay close to God.

7. Wear righteous linen. Have compassion, kindness, humility, gentleness, and patience; hold no grievances; forgive as the Lord forgives you; most of all, love one another.

8. Honor the seven feasts. It does not matter what religion you are; the God of Abraham, Isaac, and Jacob expects us to.

9. Prepare for catastrophes. Be sensible in being ready for the unexpected things to come. We were caught off guard with the plague of COVID-19; inclusively, hurricanes, floods and earthquakes are expected to get worse. There will be famines, and without the mark of the beast, you won't be able to buy food, goods, or medicine. Many will learn to trade with others for things they need. Therefore, store extra food, learn to grow your own food, and have stored water and first aid supplies.

Things You Should Not Do

1. Do not become a part of the world religious system. Don't be deceived.

2. Do not support the one world government or its leader, the Antichrist.

3. Do not take the mark of the beast. A mark, or implant, in your body that has your personal identification, which will carry the name or number of the Antichrist.

4. Do not be deceived by the news. Most news is driven by the world government, and they sensor the truth. Research for good news and resources that do not fabricate the news.

5. Do not support any agenda that is against the Bible.

6. Never curse the Holy Spirit; you will not be forgiven.

Stay close to Christian friends, neighbors, and family members. During difficult times, you must be strong in your faith and trust in our Lord, God Almighty! Before the Lord returns, you must maintain diligence, self-control, knowledge in the Word, and perseverance. The devil is going to be in control of your life. Don't let him take your soul too. Be steadfast and strong for the Lord is with you *always*. Never deny your Heavenly Father. Do not take the mark of the beast, no matter the hardships that it may bring, and pray continuously. Talk to your Heavenly Father out loud or in silence no matter what you are doing. He is with you wherever you are. Even if you lose your life in the world you are in now, you will soon have a new life in the new world that is coming.

Whatever obstacles you might face, remember God will help you through it. God will shelter you and protect you from the clasp of the evil one that walks in darkness (Ps. 91:3, 6). The Jewish belief is that before Christ's Second Coming people will go through the same plagues that the people in Egypt experienced before Moses led God's people, the Israelites, through the parted Red Sea and into the Promised Land. But the important thing you need to know is that when the plagues were released upon Egypt, God's people in Goshen were spared. The following plagues did not affect them because they were covered by the blood of the lamb:

- First plague: the rivers turned to blood; the Egyptians had no water to drink (Ex. 7:19–25).
- Second plague: frogs came up from the waters and covered the land (Ex. 8:3–15).
- Third plague: lice covered man and beast (Ex. 8:16–18).
- Fourth plague: swarms of flies covered the air and ground (Ex. 8:20–21).

   And in that day, I will set apart the land of Goshen, in which My people dwell, that no swarms of flies shall be there, in order that

you may know that I am the Lord in the
midst of the land. (Ex. 8:22 NKJV)

- Fifth plague: severe pestilence kills all livestock (cattle,
  horses, donkeys, camels, oxen, and sheep) (Ex. 9:3).

  And the Lord will make a difference
  between the livestock of Israel and the
  livestock of Egypt. So nothing shall die of
  all that belongs to the children of Israel.
  (Ex. 9:4 NKJV)

- Sixth plague: boils that become sores on man and
  beast (Ex. 9:9).
- Seventh plague: heavy hail beats down to kill every
  man, beast, and herb (Ex. 9:18–19).

  Only in the land of Goshen, where the
  children of Israel were, there was no hail.
  (Ex. 9:26 RSV)

- Eighth plague: locusts cover the earth (Ex. 10:5–6).
- Ninth plague: thick darkness for three days (Ex.
  10:21–23).

  But all the children of Israel had light in
  their dwellings. (Ex. 10:23 NKJV)

- Tenth plague: all firstborn of man and beast in the
  land of Egypt died (Ex. 11:5).

But among the Israelites not a dog will
bark at any man or animal. Then you will
know that the Lord makes a distinction
between Egypt and Israel. (Ex. 11:7 NIV)

This is when the Lord instituted Passover.

Jesus expects you to be ready and know the last days
before He comes. In Matthew 24:3–4, He says that you will
know *exactly* when He comes. The word "when" means
exactly in Hebrew, so there is no mistake in what God meant.
You should know the times and season when He is coming.
Jesus said to take heed and listen to what He tells you. You
will be deceived and believe in delusions if you do not know
the Word of God. A person can go so far offtrack by being
deceived that they will never be able to go back to where
they once were.

Know this: this is not optional. Second Timothy 3 says
that God is preparing us to know when you are in the last
days so you are not taken by surprise.

When God speaks of the last days, He is telling you of the
very end things just before He comes. Jesus is warning you
of perilous times that are full of danger. You could be hurt
or—worse—be so deceived you lose your life and eternal
life as well.

Romans 1:18–21 says that delusion will be everywhere.
You need to hold on to truth and righteousness because most
people will not want to hear about it, even though they have
heard about the truth. They do not want to glorify God or be

thankful because they enjoy living by the things Satan has to offer. They want to worship other idols, such as snakes, bugs, four-footed beasts, birds, or certain people. They dishonor their bodies with sexual perversion. First Timothy says that multitudes of people will depart from faith and will seduce spirits and morals that are not right. They will distance from the Word and, not wanting to believe, change doctrine for their own satisfaction.

Eight
THE ANTICHRIST

T he Antichrist is presently in some powerful position right now. You probably don't have any idea who he is or even might be. He does not want to be revealed until his appointed time. The Antichrist has a tremendous task of putting himself in world power to accomplish his main goal: to claim himself as God. To be able to do this, he needs to obtain the people's trust. Therefore, he will portray himself as the best leader over the world and will accomplish great things to gain your trust. Although the Antichrist will deceive most, he will not deceive God's people. This is because God's people have been told about this great deceiver and that he is the greatest deceiver that ever was or ever will be.

For you to be prepared so you will not be deceived by the evil one, you must know his characteristics. Although the Antichrist is alive today, we won't know for sure who he is until he sets himself up in the temple of God and claims to be God (referred to as *the abomination of desolation*). However, since he is the greatest deceiver of all time, you need to be knowledgeable of his characteristics so you are not deceived by him.

Throughout the Bible, there are many scriptures that tell us what to expect from this great deceiver, who is called many different names. The Antichrist is referred to as man of sin, son of perdition, wicked one, little horn, dragon, and the beast. In some scriptures, the beast is also referring to a nation or kingdom that is being ruled by an Antichrist.

> He shall seduce with flattery those who violate the covenant; but the people who know their God shall stand firm and take action. And those among the people who are wise shall make many understand, though they shall fall by sword and flame, by captivity and plunder, for some days. (Dan. 11:32–33 RSV)

The Antichrist replicates Christ in many ways. He dies by the hands of his enemy then comes back to life and does miracles. He will exalt himself and expect everyone to worship him and claims to be God. The following is a list of some of the scriptures that tell us about the Antichrist. Do not be upset, either by spirit or by word, or by anyone alleging that the day of the Lord has come. Let no one deceive you in anyway, for the day of the Lord will not come until *after* the rebellion, which comes first, and the man of lawlessness is revealed, the son of perdition. This Antichrist who opposes God and exalts himself against every so-called god or object of worship proclaims himself to be God so that he takes his seat in the temple of God (2 Thess. 2:1–4 RSV).

Many people have been misinformed by thinking that the rapture will take place before the great tribulation takes place, and they will not endure severe hardships. There are too many scriptures that state otherwise. The rapture and our Lord's Second Coming are the same event, which takes place with the last trumpet call. Christ's Second Coming will *not* take place until *after* the great tribulation, the rebellion, and the Antichrist is revealed when he takes his seat in God's temple. Is it possible that the rebellion of people comes when they realize that they are living through the great tribulation and the church did not prepare them? They will blame God for making life so terrible, and maybe if they were prepared, they would have better understood and not suffer as much. They will think God turned His back on them because they didn't think they would have to go through the great tribulation. I have noticed that too many churches have not been revealing and teaching the terrible times they will be living. The mistake some churches make is preaching that the saints will be raptured *before* the great tribulation. However, the believers *will* go through the great tribulation, but God says they will *not* endure His wrath. Remember what Jesus said in Matthew 24:29–31 (NKJV; emphasis mine),

> Immediately **after** the tribulation of those days
> the sun will be darkened, and the moon will
> not give its light; the stars will fall from heaven,
> and the powers of the heavens will be shaken.
> Then the sign of the Son of Man will appear in
> heaven, and then all the tribes of the earth will
> mourn, and they will see heaven with power
> and great glory. And He will send His angels
> with a great sound of a trumpet, and they will
> gather together His elect from the four winds,
> from one end of heaven to the other.

The Antichrist comes from among a ten-horn kingdom and will uproot three. These ten kings are the ten toes in the statue of Daniel's dream. "There before me was another horn, a little one, which came up among them; and there of the first horns were uprooted before it. This horn had eyes like the eyes of a man and a mouth that spoke boastfully" (Dan. 7:8 NIV).

"For I had seen this horn warring against God's people and winning, until the Ancient of Days came and opened his court and vindicated his people, giving them worldwide powers of government" (Dan. 7:21–22 LB).

"His ten horns are ten kings that will rise out of his empire; then another king will arise, more brutal than the other ten, and will destroy three of them" (Dan. 7:24 LB).

In these end times, the world will be experiencing major crises economically with high cost of fuel, shortages of food, and sufferings of pestilence or bioweapon. But when the Antichrist becomes the world leader, he tries to change laws and customs and succeeds in fixing the world's crisis. After he sits in the temple and claims to be God, the Antichrist will go after the saints, God's people, for three and one-half years. "He will defy the Most High God, and wear down the saints with persecution, and try to change all laws, morals, and customs. God's people will be helpless in his hands for three and a half years" (Dan. 7:25 LB).

Daniel 8:23–25 (NKJ) states that when the rebels have become completely wicked in the end part of their reign, a master of intrigue will arise. He will be a very powerful leader, but not by his own power. This strong king will succeed in whatever he does and cause massive devastation. He will destroy mighty men and God's people. He will cause deceit to prosper and will magnify and boost himself in his heart. Many will be destroyed in their prosperity, and he will even rise up against the Prince of princes but will be broken without human hand.

The Antichrist will confirm the seven-year covenant (peace agreement) with Israel and others. "He will confirm a covenant with many for one 'seven,' but in the middle of that 'seven' he will put an end to sacrifice and offering. And one who causes desolation will place abominations on a wing of the temple, until the end that is decreed is poured out on him" (Dan. 9:27 NIV). The European Union, United States, the Gulf states, and the Arab nations are a part of the Israel peace agreement. These nations have agreed to financially assist with building the desperately needed infrastructure by the West Bank, Gaza, and the sea. This peace agreement, called the Abraham Accord, was signed on August 15, 2020, by Israel and the United Arab Emirates! Now the Palestinians need to join in with a peace agreement in order to begin the final seven years.

The second beast who comes out of the earth is identified as the false prophet in Revelation 16:13 and Revelation 19:20. The false prophet performs miracles for the first beast (Antichrist). It is believed the pope will be the false prophet in the end of days. This is because he has worldwide power over the religious people and so many nations, especially those that belong to the European Union (Holy Roman Empire). Behind the pope's throne in the Papal Audience Hall in Vatican City, a statue was installed that was created by Pericle Fazzini in 1977. This work of art perversely depicts a serpent's head coming out the top of Jesus Christ. Dramatic sexual dances were performed for Pope Francis in the reptilian-shaped Vatican Hall (Geoffrey Grider, NTEB, January 8, 2020).

The Lord God says, "Abstain from all appearance of evil" (1 Thess. 5:22 KJV).

The false prophet will cause all the people in the world to worship the Antichrist who was killed and had a statue, or image, made for the people of the world to worship. The false prophet then gives life to the statue and commands all to worship him. This Antichrist who comes back to life causes everyone to have a mark of identification (666) on his right hand or forehead, or people will die if they refuse. This "666 mark" will be a microchip that will identify everything about you and have your banking codes so you will be able to buy or sell services and goods. The "image" of the Antichrist could possibly be a clone made of the beast. Today's clones are being made of certain people of wealth or hierarchy to assist in their absence or even death.

Then out of the earth came a second beast who had two horns like a lamb and it spoke like the dragon. This beast has all the power of the first beast in its presence and makes the world worship the first beast, whose deadly wound was healed. It brings fire down from heaven to earth with great signs in the sight of men. These signs were allowed to work in the presence of the beast which deceives those on earth and to create an image of the beast who was killed by the sword yet lived. The beast whose image was brought back to appear alive was given power to speak and caused those who did not want to worship the beast to be killed. It also causes all who dwell on earth, small and great, rich and poor, to be marked on their right hand or forehead so that you will not be able to buy or sell without this mark, or the number, or name of the beast. This calls for you to have wisdom: he who has understanding should know the number of this beast; for it is a human number, its number is six hundred and sixty-six. (Rev. 13:11–18 NKJV)

Children, it is the last hour; and as you have heard that antichrist is coming, so now many antichrists have come; therefore we know that it is the last hour ... But you have been anointed by the Holy One, and you all know. I write to you, not because you do not know the truth, but because you know it, and know that no lie is of the truth ... No one who denies the Son has the Father. He who confesses the Son has the Father also. Let what you heard from the beginning abide in you. If what you heard from the beginning abides in you, then you will abide in the Son and in the Father. And this is what he has promised us, eternal life. (1 John 2:18, 20, 21, 23, 24 RSV)

Although the world as we know it will soon come to an end, do not fear. For the Lord our God is going to create a new earth. We are going to live in a new world governed and led by Jesus Christ Himself!

The end of all things is near. Therefore, be clear minded and self-controlled so that you can pray. Above all, love each other deeply, because love covers over a multitude of sins.

Offer hospitality to one another without grumbling. Each one should use whatever gift he has received to serve others, faithfully administering God's grace in its various forms. (1 Pet. 4:7–10 NIV)

Nine
THE NEW WORLD

⬥⬥⬥

Hallelujah!

After God's wrath is poured out and the fall of Babylon has taken place, the heavens roar with glory!

> After this I heard what sounded like the roar of a great multitude in heaven shouting: Hallelujah! Salvation and glory and power belong to our God, for true and just are his judgments. He has condemned the great Prostitute who corrupted the earth by her adulteries. He has avenged on her the blood of His servants. (Rev. 19:1–2 NIV)

Hallelujah! For our Lord God Almighty reigns. Let us rejoice and be glad and give him glory!

> For the wedding of the Lamb has come, and his bride has made herself ready. Fine linen, bright and clean was given her to wear. Fine linen stands for the righteous acts of the saints. (Rev. 19:6–8 NIV)

An earthquake as had not occurred since men were on the earth is going to level the land.

> And there were flashes of lightning, voices, peals of thunder, and a great earthquake such as had never been since men were on the earth, so great was that earthquake. And every island fled away, and no mountains were to be found. (Rev. 16:18–20 RSV)

For God to make all things new, He has to clean up the waste and radioactive material that has been put into the earth. What better way than to "sift" the land in its entirety! And the sea will dry up from the extreme heat of the sun, fire, and nuclear scorch. But God is going to make all things new. There will be no more pain, sickness, or death. The world as we know it now will be changed to a better new world.

> "Then I saw a new heaven and a new earth, for the first heaven and the first earth had passed away, and there was no longer any sea.

I saw the Holy City, New Jerusalem, coming down out of heaven from God, prepared as a bride beautifully dressed for her husband. And I heard a loud voice from the throne saying, "Now the dwelling of God is with men, and He will dwell with them. They will be His people, and God Himself will be with them and be their God. He will wipe every tear from their eyes. There shall be no more death, or mourning, or crying, or pain, for the old order of things has passed away." He who was seated on the throne said, "I am making everything new!" (Rev. 21:1–5 NIV)

Jesus said before He was crucified that He was going to prepare a place for us and He would return to bring us to Him. He tells us in John 14:2 (KJV), "In my Father's house are many mansions; if it were not so, I would have told you. And if I go and prepare a place for you, I will come again and receive you unto myself; that where I am, there ye may be also." Well, the Lord has prepared that place for us: mansions in a glorious city with streets of gold and a river running through it. There will be no more sickness, sorrow, pain, or death. Those people chosen, the ones who lived and died for Christ, will live in this glorious Holy City that is called the New Jerusalem. The brilliantly illuminated New Jerusalem will descend out of heaven from the most gorgeous setting of clouds surrounded by the clearest intense blue skies you have ever seen. The New Jerusalem will set its foundation down to rest on a new clean and purified earth, on the Temple Mount in Israel.

> The holy Jerusalem, descending out of the skies from God. It was filled with the glory of God, and flashed and glowed like a precious gem, crystal clear like jasper. Its walls were broad and high with twelve gates guarded by twelve angels. And names of the twelve tribes of Israel were written on the gates. There were three gates on each side—north, south, east, and west. The walls had twelve foundation stones, and on them were written the names of the twelve apostles of the Lamb ... It was a square as wide as it was long: in fact it was in the form of a cube, for its height was exactly the same as its other dimensions—1,500 miles each way. Then he measured the thickness of the walls and found them to be 216 feet across (The angel called out these measurements to me, using standard units). The city itself was pure, transparent gold, like glass! The wall was made of jasper, and was built on twelve layers of foundation stones inlaid with gems: the first layers with jasper; the second with sapphire; the third with chalcedony; the fourth with emerald; the fifth with sardonyx; the sixth

layer with sardus; the seventh with chrysolite; the eighth with beryl; the ninth with topaz; the tenth with chrysoprase; the eleventh with jacinth; the twelfth with amethyst. The twelve gates were made of pearls—each gate from a single pearl! And the main street was pure, transparent gold, like glass. No temple could be seen in the city, for the Lord God Almighty and the Lamb are worshipped in it everywhere. And the city had no need of sun or moon to light it, for the glory of God and the Lamb illuminate it. Its light will light the nations of the earth, and the rulers of the world will come and bring their glory to it. Its gates never close; they stay open all day long—and there is no night! And the glory and honor of all the nations shall be brought into it. Nothing evil will be permitted in it—no one immoral or dishonest—but only those whose names are written in the Lamb's Book of Life (Rev. 21:10–27 LB).

Then the angel showed me the river of water of life, as clear as crystal, flowing from the throne of God and of the Lamb down the middle of the great street of the city. On each side of the river stood the tree of life, bearing twelve crops of fruit, yielding its fruit every month. And the leaves of the tree are for the healing of the

nations. And no longer will there be any curse.
The throne of God and of the Lamb will be in
the city, and His servants will serve Him. They
will see His face, and His name will be on their
foreheads. There will be no more night. They
will not need the light of a lamp or light of the
sun, for the Lord God will give them light.
And they will reign forever and ever. (Rev.
22:1–5 NIV)

The tree of life was in the middle of the Garden of Eden
for Adam and Eve to eat of before they were thrown out. The
tree of life is now in the New Jerusalem for all those living
there to eat of and live forever. "To him who over comes I
will give the right to eat from the tree of life, which is in
the paradise of God" (Rev. 2:7 NIV). The river of life that
proceeds from the throne of God and Jesus will be offered
to all those who thirst. "Whoever is thirsty, let him come;
and whoever wishes, let him take the free gift of the water
of life" (Rev. 22:17 NIV). "To him who is thirsty I will give
to drink without cost from the spring of the water of life. He
who overcomes will inherit all this, and I will be his God and
he will be My son" (Rev. 21:6–7 NIV).

The wolf will live with the lamb, the leopard
will lie down with the goat, the calf and the
lion and the yearling together, and a little child
will lead them. The cow will feed with the

bear, their young will lie down together, and the lion will eat straw like the ox. The infant will play near the hole of the cobra, and the young child put his hand into the viper's nest. They will neither harm nor destroy on all my holy mountain, for the earth will be full of the knowledge of the Lord as the waters cover the sea. (Isa. 11:6–9 NIV)

The people chosen to enter and live in the Holy City, the New Jerusalem, will govern over the earth in the new world under the guidance and rules set forth by the King of all kings, Jesus Christ our Lord. "But in the end the people of the Most High God shall rule the governments of the world forever and forever" (Dan. 7:18 LB).

Blessed are they that do His commandments, that they may have the right to the tree of life and may enter in through the gates into the city. For without are dogs and sorcerers and whoremongers, and murderers, and idolaters, and whosoever loveth and maketh a lie. (Rev. 22:14–15 KJV)

Before the new world comes, God will set up a government that will carry on into the new world. It will be a government that will last forever that no one can change. Of course, it won't be run by politicians; it will be governed by the chosen ones (saints) who live in the New Jerusalem. "During the reigns of those kings, the God of heaven will set up a kingdom that will never be destroyed; no one will ever conquer it. It will shatter all these kingdoms into nothingness, but it shall stand forever, indestructible" (Dan. 2:44 LB). The kingdom in the new world to come will be nothing like how we are governed today. The saints will govern the people on earth according to God's laws, equal and fair.

"And the kingdom and dominion, and the greatness of the kingdoms under the whole heaven shall be given to the people of the saints of the Most High; their kingdom shall be an everlasting kingdom, and all dominions shall serve and obey them" (Dan. 7:27 RSV).

Satan will no longer reign in God's new world. Satan will be bound for one thousand years. The saints will carry out God's rules. Our Lord and Savior, Jesus Christ, will be our superior Ruler and King.

> He seized the dragon, that ancient serpent, who is the Devil, or Satan, and bound him for a thousand years. He threw him into the Abyss, and locked and sealed it over him, to keep him from deceiving the nations any more until the thousand years were ended. (Rev. 20:2–3 NIV)

Those people who did not receive the mark of the beast (666) will reign with Jesus for the thousand years called the millennium. The millennium will be a time of peace, prosperity, purity, and prolonged life. Without Satan to create chaos and grief, we will have peace and joy!

> And I will make them and the places round about my hill a blessing; and I will send down the showers in their season; they will be showers of blessing. And the trees of the field shall yield their fruit, and the earth shall yield its increase, and they shall be secure in their land; and they shall know that I am the Lord, when I break the bars of their yoke, and deliver them from the hand of those who enslaved them. They shall no more be a prey to the nations, nor shall the beasts of the land devour them; they shall dwell securely, and none shall make them afraid. And I will provide for them prosperous plantations so that they shall no more be consumed with hunger in the land, and no longer suffer the reproach of the nations. (Ezek. 34:26–29 RSV)

> For behold, I create new heavens and a new earth; and the former things shall not be remembered or come into mind ... No more shall there be in it an infant that lives but a few days, or an old man who does not fill out his days, for the child shall die a hundred years old, and the sinner a hundred years old shall be accursed. They shall build houses and inhabit

them; they shall plant vineyards and eat their fruit. (Isa. 65:17, 20–21 RSV)

"To him who overcomes I will give the right to sit with Me on My throne, just as I overcame and sat down with My Father on His throne" (Rev. 3:21 NIV). Jesus said to them, "I tell you the truth, that in the renewal of all things, when the Son of Man sits on His glorious throne, you who have followed Me will also sit on twelve thrones, judging the twelve tribes of Israel" (Matt. 19:28 NIV). "And I assign to you, as My Father assigned to Me, a kingdom, that you may eat and drink at My table in My kingdom, and sit on thrones judging the twelve tribes of Israel" (Luke 22:29–30 RSV).

I watched as thrones were put in place and the Ancient of Days—the Almighty God—sat down to judge. His clothing was as white as snow, his hair like whitest wool. He sat upon a fiery throne brought in on flaming wheels, and a river of fire flowed from before him. Millions of angels ministered to him and hundreds of millions of people stood before him, waiting to be judged. Then the court began its session, and The Books were opened. (Dan. 7:9–10 LB)

And behold, with the clouds of heaven there came one like a son of man, and he came to the Ancient of Days and was presented before him. And to him was given dominion and glory and kingdom, that all peoples, nations, and languages, should serve him, his dominion is an everlasting dominion, which shall not pass away, and his kingdom one that shall not be destroyed. (Dan. 7:13–14 RSV)

And there before me was a throne in heaven with someone sitting on it. And the one who sat there had the appearance of jasper and a carnelian. A rainbow, resembling an emerald, encircled the throne. Surrounding the throne were twenty-four elders. They were dressed in white and had crowns of gold on their heads. And from the throne came flashes of lightning, rumblings and peals of thunder. Before the throne, seven lamps were blazing. These are the seven spirits of God. (Rev. 4:2–5 NIV)

And the twenty-four elders, who were seated on their throne before God, fell on their face and worshiped God saying: We give thanks to you, Lord God Almighty, who is and who was, because you have taken your great power and have begun to reign. The nations were angry, and your wrath has come, the time has come for judging the dead, and rewarding your servants the prophets and your saints, and those who reverence your name, both small and great—and for destroying those who destroy the earth. Then God's temple in heaven was opened, and within his temple was seen the ark of his covenant. And there came flashes of lightning, rumblings, peals of thunder, an earthquake, and great hailstorm. (Rev. 11:16–19 NIV)

Then I saw thrones, and seated on them were those to whom judgment was committed. Also I saw the souls of those who had been beheaded for their testimony to Jesus and for the word of God, and who had not worshiped the beast or its image and had not received its mark on the foreheads or their hands. They came to life, and reigned with Christ a thousand years. The rest of the dead did not come to life until the thousand years were ended. This is the first resurrection. Blessed and holy is he who shares in the first resurrection! Over such the second death has no power, but they shall be priests of God and of Christ, and they shall reign with him a thousand years. (Rev. 20:4–6 RSV)

There will be a time of judgment. A time when the King of kings decides on whether to blot your name from the Lamb's Book of Life or allow you to live and reign with Him forever. "He who overcomes will, like them, be dressed in white. I will never erase his name from the book of life, but will acknowledge his name before My Father and before His angels" (Rev. 3:5 NIV).

> And I saw the dead, small and great, standing before the throne, and books were opened. Another book was opened, which is the Book of Life. The dead were judged according to what they had done as recorded in the books. The sea gave up the dead who were in it, and death and Hades gave up the dead that were in them, and each person was judged according to what he had done. Then death and Hades were thrown into the lake of fire. The lake of fire is the second death. If anyone's name is not found written in the book of life, he was thrown into the lake of fire. (Rev. 20:12–15 NIV)

> In him you also, who have heard the word of truth, the gospel of your salvation, and have believed in him, were sealed with the promised Holy Spirit, which is the guarantee of our inheritance until we acquire possession of it, to the praise of his glory. (Eph. 1:13–14 RSV)

> And you he made alive, when you were dead through the trespasses and sins in which you once walked, following the course of this world, following the prince of the power of the

air, the spirit that is now at work in the sons of disobedience. Among these we all once lived in the passions of flesh, following the desires of body and mind, and so we were by nature children of wrath, like the rest of humankind. But God, who is rich in mercy, out of the great love with which He loved us, even when we were dead through our trespasses, made us alive together with Christ (by grace you have been saved), and raised us up with Him, and made us sit with Him in the heavenly places in Christ Jesus, that in the coming ages he might show the immeasurable riches of his grace in kindness toward us in faith; and this is not your own doing, it is the gift of God—not because of works, lest any man should boast. (Eph. 2:1–9 RSV)

Ten
ENTERING THE KINGDOM OF GOD

U pon the time of conception, when your physical body first began to grow inside your mother's womb, your body was designed to die only one time. Our physical bodies, also known as "flesh," are born once and they die once. However, God also designed our bodies to have a spirit. You cannot physically see one's spirit. It is not of bones and flesh. Your spirit is the "breath of life" within you. Although there are many different spirits, there is only one good and righteous spirit, which is the Holy Spirit of God. To enter the kingdom of God, you must be "born again." "In reply Jesus declared: I tell you the truth, unless a man is born again, he cannot see the kingdom of God" (John 3:3 NIV). When a person is born again, he has been renewed or changed in spirit because he has been baptized in water and has received the Holy Spirit of God by accepting our Lord Jesus into his heart.

> Jesus answered, **"I tell you the truth, unless a man is born of water and the Spirit, he cannot enter the kingdom of God. Flesh gives birth to flesh, but the Spirit gives birth to spirit."** (John 3:5–6 NIV; emphasis mine)

It takes more than just believing in God to go to heaven and live in His kingdom. For even the devil, Satan, believes in God and His existence. Satan was once God's chosen angel. But when Satan wanted to rule over God and not live God's way, God threw Satan out of heaven. "I saw Satan fall like lightning from heaven" (Luke 10:18 NIV). "The great dragon was hurled down—that ancient serpent called the Devil or Satan, who leads the whole world astray. He was hurled to the earth and his angels with him" (Rev. 12:9 NIV). God says it takes more than just believing to live. "As the body without the spirit is dead, so faith without deeds is dead" (James 2:26 NIV).

If you do not have the Holy Spirit of God, you cannot

enter the kingdom of God. This is because the Holy Spirit lives with God forever; the Holy Spirit *is* God. Those people who do not choose to accept Jesus as the Son of God and are not born again of the Holy Spirit will not enter the Holy City, God's kingdom. Only the Holy Spirit lives forever. All other spirits die. Man dies a physical death, and man will die a second death if he does not possess the Spirit of God. If you do not have the Spirit of God living within you at the time of your physical death, your spirit will die by spending eternity in the lake of fire, also known as hell. "But the cowardly, the unbelieving, the vile, the murderers, the sexually immoral, those who practice magic arts, the idolaters, and all liars— their place will be in the fiery lake of burning sulfur. This is the second death" (Rev. 21:8 NIV).

Remember this: you must never speak out against the Holy Spirit, or you will not be forgiven. "Anyone who speaks a word against the Son the Man will be forgiven, but anyone who speaks against the Holy Spirit will not be forgiven, either in this age or in the age to come" (Matt. 12:32 NIV).

> Do you not know that the unrighteous will not inherit the kingdom of God? Do not be deceived; neither the immoral, nor idolaters, nor adulterers, nor sexual perverts, nor thieves, nor the greedy, nor drunkards, nor revilers, nor robbers will inherit the kingdom of God. (1 Cor. 6:9–10 RSV)

During these times of trouble, it will be exceptionally hard, but you must remain loyal to God and stand up for the Son of Man, our Lord Christ Jesus. If not, you will lose the right to enter the Holy City—the kingdom of God. The Lord only asks for us to live for Him now. However, you will have to die for Him if you are left behind after the rapture takes place. It is going to be hard to remain faithful to God because most people are going to be deceived by Satan—those who choose to believe the lies of Satan instead of the truth of God.

> The coming of the lawless one will be in accordance with the work of Satan displayed in all kinds of counterfeit miracles, signs and wonders, and in every sort of evil that deceives those who are perishing. They perish because they refused to love the truth and so be saved. For this reason, God sends them a powerful delusion so that they will believe the lie and so that all will be condemned who have not believed the truth but have delighted in wickedness. But we ought always to thank God for you, brothers loved by the Lord, because God from the beginning chose you to be saved through sanctifying work the Spirit and through belief in the truth. (2 Thess. 2:9–13 NIV)

Hold on to faith that our Lord and King will return in power and great glory to reward you with everlasting life, to live with Him in the New Jerusalem and eat from the tree of life.

> But the day of the Lord will come as a thief. The heavens will disappear with a roar; the elements will be destroyed by fire; and the earth and everything in it will be laid bare. Since everything will be destroyed in this way, what kind of people ought you to be? You ought to live holy and godly lives as you look forward to the day of God and speed its coming. That day will bring about destruction of the heavens by fire, and the elements will melt in the heat. But in keeping with his promise, we are looking forward to a new heaven and a new earth, the home of righteousness. (2 Pet. 3:10–13 NIV)

This is what you must know and do to get into heaven:

- Jesus answered, "I am the way and the truth and the life. No one comes to the Father except through me." (John 14:6 NIV)
- For there is one God and one Mediator between God and men, the Man Christ Jesus. (1 Tim. 2:5 RSV)
- If you confess with your mouth, "Jesus is Lord" and believe in your heart that God raised Him from the dead, you will be saved. (Rom. 10:9 NIV)

- Jesus answered him, "Truly, truly, I say to you, unless one is born of water and the Spirit, he cannot enter the kingdom of God." (John 3:5 RSV)
- No one who believes in him will be put to shame ... For, everyone who calls upon the name of the Lord will be saved. (Rom. 10:11, 13 RSV)

Lord Jesus, please come into my heart.
Please forgive me of my sins, and
show me how to be the kind of person You want me to be.
I believe You died on the cross and rose again.
I love You and want to worship You forever.
Thank You, oh God, for loving me. Amen.

Works Cited

Internet: Israel Ministry of Foreign Affairs, Declaration of Establishment of State of Israel, 1948.

www.mfa.gov.il/mfa/foreignpolicywww.mfa.gov.il/foreignpolicy.

Endtime Ministries, Baxter, Seven Year Peace Covenant (television broadcast), 2016.

www.Study.com Markey, Dell, What Does Red in Communism Mean?, 2001.

www.classroom.synonym.com.

Capitalism. https://en.wikipedia.org.

World War II. https://en.wikipedia.org.

Endtime Ministries, Baxter, Chernobyl Prophecy Come to Light, 2001.

http://www.endtime.com/endtime-magazine-articles/chernobyl-shuts-down/.

Geoffrey Grider, NTEB (January 8, 2020), https://www.naturalnews.com/2020-01-29-false-prophet-pope-francis-hosts-bizarre-drag-queen-circus-reptilian-shaped-vatican-hall.html.

Lalit K. Jha, Israel, UAE, and Bahrain Sign Abraham Accord, September 16, 2020.

Printed in the United States
by Baker & Taylor Publisher Services